T0058259

The
Problem with
PERFECT

*How to Shift Your Focus to
Find Your Purpose*

Bo Parrish

WESTBOW®
PRESS
A DIVISION OF THOMAS NELSON
& ZONDERVAN

WestBow Press books may be ordered through booksellers or by contacting:

WestBow Press
A Division of Thomas Nelson & Zondervan
1663 Liberty Drive
Bloomington, IN 47403
www.westbowpress.com
1 (866) 928-1240

ISBN: 978-1-4908-6366-5 (sc)
ISBN: 978-1-4908-6365-8 (hc)
ISBN: 978-1-4908-6364-1 (e)

Library of Congress Control Number: 2015900481

Print information available on the last page.

WestBow Press rev. date: 04/16/2015

CONTENTS

INTRODUCTION

My Personal Story

What could possibly be wrong with perfection? According to Mr. Webster, there is no greater thing, so why would I write a book about the problems associated with perfection? Let me set the record straight before I even begin. *This book will not be perfect!* Perfection is a stone-cold killer, caring nothing about its pursuers until it's too late. I spent many years chasing it until it finally dropped me in an emergency room where I slipped into a coma, fighting for my life. The problem with perfection is that it is not possible, and thinking otherwise could lead you to your demise. How do I know? Well, I'd like to share a story about my journey back to life and an invaluable lesson I learned along the way. If I would have known then what I know now, there would be no story to tell. If you're still not convinced and believe perfection is the goal of life no matter the cost, I wish you well, but my heart breaks for what lies ahead on your path. It may not be tomorrow or the next day or even ten years from now, but ultimately your pursuit of perfection will end in devastation. I'll share a brief account of my personal experience to make my point, but the purpose of this book is to illustrate the impossibility of perfection while we define a clear path that will lead you to your purpose. I do not wish my experience on my worst enemy, so please don't wait as long as I did to discover this realization; your life may depend on it.

At the age of thirteen. I was diagnosed with a chronic illness that

I allowed to destroy my physical body. Crohn's disease stole half of my life and ultimately forced me to fight to get it back. The irony all along is that I could have easily overcome the pain and suffering I endured by electing to undergo the surgery that was recommended multiple times along the way. I always resisted strongly, because I saw surgery as a threat, an intrusion into my personal comfort zone. I would be left with an external appliance that would take the place of my diseased colon. I would live as a freak with a poop bag attached to the outside of my body. This image horrified me as a teenager, and therefore, surgery became my arch enemy. I convinced myself that any amount of pain was better than that bag, and even though my pain grew worse by the day, it was my picture of perfect. I spent the better part of my high school and collegiate years as the sick kid who missed out on most social events. My colon eventually ruptured and surgery became my only option—that is, of course, if I wanted to live. On that fateful day in 2006 when I slipped out of consciousness, I finally realized that perfection was not possible and that my life was now in jeopardy because I'd insisted otherwise for so long. After a complicated recovery that lasted more than four months, I discovered my passion, which led me to my purpose. The problem with perfection, I found, is that the impossibility has the potential to result in paralysis. My plan was to pursue my perception of what the perfect life might be, one with my insides fully intact. Thank goodness life doesn't always go as planned. I am so grateful to realize now that I will never be perfect!

There is no such thing as perfection, but is that necessarily a bad thing? Nothing in life lasts forever. Change happens and can be the difference between thriving and merely surviving. Most people are creatures of habit. We are attracted to what is familiar and establish routines to protect against uncertainty. We seek personal comfort and avoid anything that could potentially interrupt the status quo. The problem with this mind-set is that it can easily lead to mediocrity and obscurity. We rob ourselves of potential greatness because of our fear of the unknown. We do what is necessary to get by rather than taking chances that could lead to breakthroughs. Unfortunately, we cannot change the fact that our lives will change. The opportunity comes with our perception of and reaction *to* change. It is not a temporary inconvenience but a blessing in disguise. If we could bring ourselves to see beyond the initial inconvenience and focus on the possibilities, the trajectory of most of our lives would be drastically different.

I am confident that we would experience more innovation, healthier lifestyles complete with collaboration, and a better sense of overall well-being. Here's the thing though. You have to be willing to become uncomfortable and act against your instinct to even give yourself a chance to be great. That's right. The best version of you waits on the other side of change. As a survivor of a near-death experience, I can tell you that life is so much sweeter on the other side of change. The problem with perfection is that it just doesn't matter. You're the only one who cares and even thinks it's possible. How could something be so obvious to every other person around you yet so hard for you to grasp? Well, if you're willing to risk your life to chase perfection, I guess it really doesn't matter what I have to say— except for the fact that I did, yet lived to share this story.

The most amazing thing that I have learned in this life is that I am not perfect. I know it sounds ridiculously obvious, but it took a near-death experience for me to realize it. If there is one thing you take away from this book, please hear me when I say, "You are not perfect, *but* you don't have to be." I lost thirteen years of life chasing perfection. My selfish pursuit of the impossible led me into a coma after I experienced septic shock. I'd fought hard to achieve perfection, but my body fought against me. I am fortunate to be alive and will not pretend for another moment that perfection is possible.

In a world that promotes perfection, it is difficult to see beyond ourselves. We are bombarded with self-promotion messages that cause us to view perfection as possible. Facebook, Twitter, Instagram—there are no shortages of opportunities for us to project our manufactured perfection. The problem with social media is that we don't post reality. Remember, we chase perfection as is if it's possible. We strive, we grind, and for what? The approval of the world around us? Let me assure you that the end of that road will offer nothing more than frustration and disappointment. Perfection is a lonely path that leads to destruction. Life is too short to be focused on perfection! Unfortunately, you're the only one who doesn't see it.

Purpose and perfection are not exactly a great pair. As human beings, we are created for a purpose —but not for perfection. Purpose is not only possible, but is essential for a life of meaning and significance. It took me far too long to come to this realization, and I will not spend another minute pretending that perfection is possible. After a catastrophic failure, my eyes and my soul have been opened to the process of purpose. I am fully aware that not everyone can relate to a near-death experience, but I do think everyone struggles with the illusion of perfection. If you want to live the rest of your days in isolation and frustration, by all means keep at it. If, on the other hand, you long to discover your unique purpose in life, then I encourage you to walk this path to purpose. There are specific steps on the path to purpose, and they are all imperfect; however, they don't have to be. This is a story about purpose and it won't be perfect. But I now am living my passion and I would like to offer you the confidence that will help you see that you can too, even if it takes starting over (and over) until you do! Life is not a solo journey and you are not in control. Your purpose is a process, but the end result is as close to perfect as your life will ever be. I trust you will consider and implement these steps in your own life and that you will never be fearful of starting over, no matter how long it takes for you to discover your purpose. If I can do it, anyone can!

CHAPTER 1

The Killer Called Perfection

Have no fear of perfection. You'll never reach it.

—Salvador Dalí

The need for perfection comes in many different flavors, each with its own set of problems. I am going to analyze three key areas of life where perfection kills: self-worth, relationships, and body image. Perfection will paralyze your potential, ruin your relationships, and break your body.

I am happy to say that I survived my pursuit of perfection. It was a hard-fought battle, and I nearly lost; however, in the end I snatched victory from the jaws of defeat. I am living the message of this book and now feel the need to share a bit of insight to give others a greater perspective. For thirteen years I believed a lie that my body was stronger than it really was. I was diagnosed with Crohn's disease as a young teenager. This rare digestive disorder declared war on my life and slowly but surely wore me down. Eventually my digestive tract became so weak that I needed surgery to remove my large intestine. This meant I would require an ileostomy. I would live the rest of my days as a freak with a poop bag that was visible for all to see. This was not a life-threatening situation, but I would have rather died than have the operation. So I resisted surgery, even though I knew it would drastically improve the quality of my life. My days were filled with pain beyond imagination, but in my own sick mind, life was perfectly predictable. I was hanging on for dear life, yet I maintained control. Between the ages of thirteen and twenty-five, surgery was recommend to me on three separate occasions. I made surgery my enemy and ultimately lost the battle.

On March 30, 2006, I was faced with a decision I thought I would never have to make. The night was cold and wet as I slipped in and out of consciousness. An ambulance had arrived at the hotel where I was staying to rush me to the emergency room. For the past six hours I had been fighting—and losing—against my body. Unbeknownst to me, my colon had ruptured and I was becoming more and more septic by the minute. My abdomen was so distended that I could have easily been mistaken for a pregnant father ready to give birth. The bacteria in my bloodstream were causing my skin to become discolored, and the pain was more than I could bear. I remember wishing that I would pass out and slip into a coma—anything to deliver me from what was happening. I was shivering and running a fever, and I just knew I was going to die. The paramedics tried to keep me conscious, but their efforts were largely wasted. The drive from the hotel to the hospital could not have been more than ten miles; however, we were in Nowheresville, Canada, and the roads were dark and narrow.

The ambulance came to a sudden stop, and before I knew it, I was being wheeled furiously through the entrance and down the dimly lit hall to the emergency room. I was lying on the stretcher flat on my back, paralyzed with pain; I could see my abdomen protruding from my core. I noticed a man in a white coat standing next to my makeshift bed. As the doctor examined my traumatized body, I felt more and more like death was upon me. The surgeon spoke, but I heard nothing. He tried desperately to get my attention, as he needed my consent for the miracle he was about to perform. All I could hear was a faint murmur, and I suddenly felt a sharp pain on my left arm. A needle penetrated my skin and made its way to my bloodstream. That pain medicine was incredible.

The morphine now freely flowed inside of me, providing a temporary but welcome relief. The doctor explained that my colon had ruptured and that he would need to operate immediately. He did not actually tell me I would die, but I knew my life was coming to an end. For a split second I allowed my mind to wander toward death. I remember thinking I'd lived a good life with no regrets. I have to admit that I did entertain the thought of death, if for no other reason than to escape the pain. My mind raced. Death was for old people, certainly not me. I could not speak; I simply nodded my head when I was spoken to. I was then handed a telephone, and could hear my parents' voices on the other end. I'm not sure if I even heard what they were trying to tell me, but whatever it was they convinced me that my life must go on. My life had been too short to die then. I had many more things to do, people to meet, and places to see. I wanted to have a family one day. It's incredible what a near-death experience will do for a mind in terms of perspective. I wasn't supposed to be here; I was young with many years ahead of me. There was just one slight problem: my colon had been torn open from years of inflammation and scarring.

My mind quickly snapped back to reality as I realized the doctor was staring at me, waiting for an answer. I raised a thumb, and a crew of hospital staff rolled me quickly into the operating room. My surgeon had quite a job to do. Because I was so sick, I was completely self-absorbed. I could have avoided arriving at this point; all I had to do was surrender to the surgery and realize my imperfection years before. I was given three chances to do so, but no, I was bound and determined to suffer if it allowed me to hold on to my perfection. If left to my own selfish design, I would not be alive to share this story.

From the depths of my heart, I hope that you have not had a similar experience, but I do not feel such an experience is necessary to benefit from this message. Perfection will wreck your life. Trust me. I've experienced it. At the same time I believe there is incredible irony in this notion. Consider the world in which we live and then your own view of perfection. Progress and accomplishment at any cost are handsomely rewarded. Not only does society promote perfection, but it also encourages us with messages like "anything is possible." What we often fail to realize or ignore is the cost that comes along with these. Relationships, health, mental clarity—these are the things that are compromised on the path to perfect. Sadly, these costs are too often tolerated and labeled as side effects. They can even be ignored altogether or rationalized as acceptable. As you pursue your perfect life, you will neglect the truly important things in life. You are not alone, and your decisions impact those who are close to you. A life bent toward perfection is a life destined for heartache, not only for you but also for those around you. After all, what's the point of perfection if you have no one to share it with?

If you could paint the picture of perfection for your life, what would it look like? Most likely you would envision a result of some effort sustained over a period of time. Maybe it's money, and you imagine no longer having to worry about it. Maybe it's fame, and you are celebrated everywhere you go. Maybe it's power and accomplishment, and you control the financial well-being of thousands of people. Let me ask you one more thing: Would your perfect picture have anyone other than you at the center? If you are anything like me, the answer to that question is no. Your quest for perfection demands all your time, energy, and emotion. You are tenacious beyond reason, and anyone who interferes is a threat. Now consider this same scenario, but this time think about if I asked your loved ones—your spouse, your children, or even a close friend, to draw the picture of your perfect life. Would they say the same thing? Perfection lies in the eye of the beholder. It is impossible for perfection to reach consistency in relationships because of its self-centered focus. Your pursuit of perfection will clash with the desires of those whom you love.

According to an article by Dr. Shauna Springer in *Psychology Today*, the strong traits of perfectionist personalities usually prevent the formation of healthy relationships. Dr. Springer explains that perfectionists do not experience a full range of emotions but rather vacillate between dread and relief. Perfectionists spend most of their time dreading the next potential failure, and temporary success is met with short-term relief. In addition, perfectionists feel as if they must be strong and constantly in control. Spouses of perfectionists often comment on their partners' emotional unavailability because of the avoidance of talking about personal fears, inadequacies, and insecurities. When caught up in the bondage that accompanies the pursuit of perfection, a person is much less likely to care about cultivating an intimate relationship. If you are going to chase perfection, you must be willing to sacrifice your relationships.[1]

Let's consider another area of life that is hurt by the pursuit of perfection—body image. Your body is a gift, and you only get one. Your body is unique and unlike any other and requires your care and attention. This particular area is the one that I struggle with to this day. Body image over body well-being is the focal point in society today. We see beauty everywhere we look, and we are very quick to compare ourselves to what we see. The images before us are perfect, and the world promotes that perfection, so we pursue it. What we don't see is the cost; we never do. We look beyond the process and focus on the result. We see it as possible because it has already been done. The idea that we can reshape our bodies in order to live better lives is devastating.

I'm not talking about nutrition and exercise. These are necessities in life. What I am referring to is the battle within. Pain with this pursuit is a wonderful thing, as it hints of oncoming danger. Pain is a natural response our bodies give us when something is wrong. When we heed the warning and explore the potential causes, we are acting consistently with the ongoing care that our bodies require for longevity. When pain is ignored or tolerated beyond reasonable measure, things become dangerous. When we compromise our health and bodies to pursue a certain body image, perfection rears its ugly head. To this day I struggle with my body image. The thing that I dreaded most in life is now a reality: I live with a permanent ileostomy, and the whole world can see it. I have an everlasting reminder of my catastrophic failure and defeat. I have a medical device that sits on the surface of my abdomen that collects bodily waste. I also have a nine-inch scar from the night

---

1 http://www.psychologytoday.com/blog/the-joint-adventures-well-educated-couples/201209/how-perfectionism-hurts-relationships

my surgeon opened me up for my emergency procedure. The surgery defeated me, and I cannot hide the physical evidence. What I fail to realize far too often is that these bodily alterations are my signs of life. I am extremely vulnerable in this area and have tremendous compassion for body-image battles.

The world is our enemy because it tricks us into believing that we can have perfect bodies. The pursuit starts with an idea, which gives birth to action. Action leads to habit, which paves the way for addiction. Addiction leads to isolation, which ultimately creates disappointment, frustration, and permanent damage. Body image is an epidemic of catastrophic proportions. For some reason we convince ourselves that if we can manage to look a certain way, we will feel that much better. The picture of perfection exists in our minds, and as a result, we set ridiculous expectations. We take good things like nutrition and exercise and turn them into obsessions. According to a recent article featured in *Healthline*, Heaven Stubblefied defines exercise addiction as "an unhealthy obsession with physical fitness and exercise. It is often a result of body image disorders and eating disorders. Exercise addicts display traits similar to those of other addicts. These include obsession with the behavior, engaging in the behavior even though it is causing physical harm, engaging in the behavior despite wanting to stop, and engaging in the behavior in secret."[2] This is a problem, but the only one who cannot see it for what it really is … is you. And for that matter, the only one who really cares is you. You are putting your body in serious jeopardy and damaging your longevity. Exercise addiction is often accompanied by eating disorders. Once again the pursuit of that perfect body image is the primary driver. Statistics taken from the National Eating Disorder Association (NEDA) reveal that in the United States, twenty million women and ten million men suffer from a clinically significant eating disorder at some time in their lives. Whether it's by eating or exercise, the pursuit of your perfect body image can destroy you.[3]

---

2 http://www.healthline.com/health/exercise-addiction#Overview1
3 https://www.nationaleatingdisorders.org/get-facts-eating-disorders

Relationships and body image are obvious areas where perfectionists can struggle. Not so apparent (at least to the outside world) is the personal battle with progress. As human beings, we were created for adventure with daring imaginations. I mean, how many skeptical kids do you run into every day? We have much to learn from children. Think about your own early childhood and your perception of the world. We dreamed of becoming superheroes and professional athletes and presidents of countries. We were expert storytellers full of creativity. We lived with confidence and carried aspirations of grandeur. Nothing was impossible, and we were limited only by the scope of our imaginations. All of a sudden we grow up. It is an utterly catastrophic yet undeniable fact of life that our imaginations shrink as our bodies grow. As we mature both physically and emotionally, we begin to develop an awareness of the world around us. We start to think about the future, and our dreams become smaller. We begin to hear things like "don't be silly" or "grow up" or even "get real." Our hope and childlike faith are replaced by practicality and rationale. Our perception of reality grows beyond the present day, and we learn how to worry about things over which we have no control. We compare our day-to-day lives with the highlight reels of celebrity. Our social circles expand, and we begin to meet people who have been pushed down by the world. We learn about what it means to grow old. We feel pressure and responsibility and develop new beliefs about who we really are. Our minds, which were once filled with imagination and bright ideas, become clouded with daily tasks and to-do lists. We learn about failure and disappointment and discover unrealistic expectations that others place upon us. We give birth to a tiny voice inside our heads that nags, scolds, and taunts. All of a sudden we are older, and our creativity has evaded us.

As we continue to grow into adulthood, the child within us diminishes. We develop habits that lead to routines that ultimately leave us empty. We begin to long for something more, and oftentimes we cannot figure it out. We develop new vocabularies and learn to say things like *why* and *can't* and *won't*. We assign ourselves limits and develop comfort zones that we dare not stray from. We lose our senses of adventure in favor of what is normal. We accept rather than challenge. We suppress rather than vocalize. We blend in rather than stand out, and slowly but surely we allow life to push us down. We get by and simply endure rather than thrive. We do as little as possible, or the bare minimum of what is required. We lose conviction and motivation to excel. Over the years we grow cold, suspicious, and pessimistic. As we encounter troubles in life, we recognize them as proof of heartache and demise. We begin to see others as threats and defend ourselves relentlessly. We develop an instinct that we feel is necessary to protect ourselves from ever getting hurt again. We trade our vulnerability for cold harsh reality. We spend the majority of our lives trading our time for money and in most cases despise the substance of what we call work. We grind through every day. We hold on, looking forward only to the weekend, which presents a momentary break from our realities. At some point along the way we begin to calculate our time until we no longer have to work anymore. I guess most would call this day retirement, but then it's really just more of the same, isn't it? As human beings, we were created to thrive, yet anything short of perfection elicits failure. We trade our childlike faith and determination for mediocrity and obscurity because it involves less effort. We justify our resignation by assuring ourselves that we tried and that life just isn't fair.

We were all created with the desire to make an impact and to leave the world better than when we came. This impact does not have to be profound nor does it have to be a brilliant innovation. Perfection is not the goal, but then again it never should have been. Perfection paves the way for failure before you ever get started. Perfection taunts and belittles. Hey, I have been trying to write this book now for six years! Why isn't it finished yet? I wish I could answer that question. I'm sad to say it's taken me this long to come to the realization that my perfection does you no good. For six years my thoughts have remained my own and thus were not shared. I believe in my heart of hearts that I was born to write this book. I believe my life was spared to share this message. Why in the world would I feel that it needed to be perfect? This is the struggle I face, and I bet you've experienced it too.

Perfectionism is procrastination, and it can be devastating to your potential. Undeveloped potential is wasted talent. What good is an idea in your head if it never becomes a reality? An idea without action is as useful as a teacher with no voice. You could be carrying the cure to cancer, and the world would never know because you never shared. It's not that you don't want to help, but that you are afraid of what might happen if your idea doesn't work. You are more concerned about perfecting your idea than sharing your idea. Along the way, you could unknowingly be depriving the world of exactly what it needs, whatever that might be.

I can think of three pioneers who revolutionized the world in which we live. None of these men were perfect, and all experienced failure and criticism along the way. Can you image a world without electricity? Neither could Thomas Edison, and his determination paved the way for modern-day technology. In December 1879, after a year and half of work, Edison successfully revealed the incandescent electric light. Thomas Edison's teachers said he was "too stupid to learn anything." He was fired from his first two jobs for being unproductive. Edison made a thousand unsuccessful attempts at inventing the lightbulb. When a reporter asked, "How did it feel to fail a thousand times?" Edison replied, "I didn't fail a thousand times. The lightbulb was an invention with a thousand steps." What about a world devoid of cinematic entertainment? Walt Disney created more than eighty-one feature films and hundreds of shorts. He earned more than 950 honors, including forty-eight Academy Awards. He founded the California Institute of the Arts. And he built Disneyland. And through Walt Disney Productions, the Disney name became one of the most famous and trusted brands in the world, but his path was far from perfect.[4] Disney had great potential, and like Edison, he was determined to share his conviction with the world even in the face of opposition. According to Hollywoodstories. com, Disney formed his first animation company in Kansas City in

---

4 http://www.mouseplanet.com/9365/
Of_Failure_and_Success_The_Journey_of_Walt_Disney

1921. He made a deal with a distribution company in New York in which he would ship them his cartoons and get paid six months down the road. He was forced to dissolve his company, and at one point he could not pay his rent and was surviving by eating dog food. Far from perfect. Lastly, consider the legacy of Steve Jobs. In August 2012, Apple overtook Microsoft as the largest company in the world. Apple hit the new milestone—Disney lion—at a time when its influence on the economy, on the stock market, and on popular culture rivaled that of some of the most powerful companies in US history.[5] Not bad for a guy who was fired from the very same company twenty-seven years prior. There was nothing perfect about the early pursuits of these three men. Each came to grips with their imperfection and persevered in the face of adversity. I don't know about you, but I'm sure glad the ideas of Edison, Disney, and Jobs made it out of their minds and into the world!

If the lives of these three men do not provide adequate evidence that perfection is not necessary for success and significance, I don't know how else to further communicate my message. The world is our greatest enemy, but we have a powerful choice. The trajectory of our futures is dependent not on perfection but on purpose. Perfection is impossible. I hope that much is clear by now. The impacts of Edison, Disney, and Jobs were nothing short of spectacular, and the world will forever be grateful; however, they were not perfect people. What made these men heroic was their discovery of purpose.

Up to this point we have examined the problems associated with perfection. Now that you are well aware of the problem, the remainder of this story will deal with the solution. Remember, you were not created for perfection and no one expects it. You were, however, created for a purpose, and the sooner you find it, the better off the world will be. Think of your purpose as an integral piece of a puzzle. As human beings who are social in nature, we were created for fellowship. There are no two people in the world today whose purpose is identical. Much like

5 http://online.wsj.com/news/articles/SB10000872396390443855804577601773524745182

our physical bodies, we function better as a whole with complementary actions. Not only will your discovery of purpose in life benefit you, but those around you will be better off as well. Purpose is a selfless pursuit that leads to meaning and significance in life. What I have learned in the years since my life-saving surgery is what I intend to reveal in this book. The best part about my dance with death is that I am now living a life I never thought was possible. If there is any gap between the life you live now and the one you want to live, my hope is that you stick with me and walk the path of the purpose process. Wherever you are, it's never too late. Your purpose is out there and desires desperately to be found. You need to get started, and you may have to start over (and over and over again); however, you will find your passion, and the purpose of the rest of this book is to take you there.

CHAPTER 2

Wave the White Flag

The greatness of the man's power is the measure of his surrender.

—William Booth

Do you remember the scene from the all-American movie *Rocky IV* when Ivan Drago stares down at Apollo Creed just before the match and utters, "You will lose…?" In that moment you knew that Apollo had no chance of winning. Drago was stronger, faster, and as evidenced by those eerie words, more confident (despite Apollo's opening circus act). The bout starts tamely with Apollo landing several punches that have no effect on the Russian. It soon turns serious though as Drago beats Apollo mercilessly. Apollo is in critical condition by the end of the first round. Rocky and Apollo's trainer pleads with him to give up, but Apollo refuses to do so and tells Rocky not to stop the fight. The second round doesn't go any better, but Rocky honors Apollo's request by not throwing in the towel. This turns out to have fatal consequences, as Drago beats Apollo to the point where he falls and dies in the ring. In the immediate aftermath Drago displays no sense of remorse, commenting to the assembled media, "If he dies … he dies."

This is the picture of your battle with perfection. I often wonder if Apollo would have even gotten in the ring if he had known the power of Drago ahead of time? Had he known that his life was in jeopardy, would he have continued beyond the first round? Perfection is a fight you can't win. It's an enemy that can't be defeated. All the determination and effort you can muster is not enough to overcome imperfection. So are you ready to surrender? Are you ready to wave your white flag?

Whether or not you agree with what I've shared thus far, do you think you can find peace in the face of imperfection? Insanity is doing the same thing over and over and expecting the result to change. Until you are ready to surrender to imperfection, you are not ready to continue. As a matter of fact, I would encourage you to stop reading. There is nothing of meaning I can share because your mind is closed. I know I can lead you to water, but I cannot stick your face in and make you drink; I cannot make you thirsty if you're not. I cannot open your mind to share the wisdom I've obtained on my journey back to life if it's closed. You might not be in a place to hear this message, and that's okay. But it's not okay to stay that way. The sooner you open your mind to the possibility of finding your purpose and the sooner you let go of perfection, the better your life will be for you and those you love. If you're still reading, I will surmise that you're with me and get on with the story because your white flag has indeed been waved.

Surrender is so sweet yet so unnatural. It goes against everything the world tells us. What comes to mind when you contemplate surrender? I must admit upon first consideration, my thoughts were associated with weakness, frailty, and passivity. These were the feelings I carried for so long as I fought the symptoms of my sickening body. My experience as a terribly sick kid led to bitterness and resentment. My mind had declared war on my disease, and my body suffered because of it. I viewed surgery as defeat, which ultimately led to the emergency that nearly claimed my life. I was living a lie, but because my mind was calling the shots, my body had no choice but to follow.

Surrender really is a matter of perception that is rooted in control. To a certain extent, we all desire control, which is a clear sign of our pursuit of perfection. When we perceive surrender as weak, our instinct leads to resistance. I chose pain and suffering because it was predictable. Surgery was a gamble. It was something that presented uncertainty and a potential lack of control. At the precise time it could have helped me,

I fought it the hardest. My refusal to surrender to the unknown kept me bound to my predictably painful existence. Fortunately for me, my surrender was not a choice; I did not have the luxury of continuing the fight and I resisted to the point of death. How pathetic was I! It wasn't until after my life-saving surgery that I came to the realization that I had surrendered a battle so that I might win the war. I was fighting against an Ivan Drago, believing I had what it took to win. I say it again—how pathetic was I!

The battle with perfection is not a battle at all. If you pursue it, you will lose—and not because you are weak or ill-prepared but because the battle does not exist. How silly would Apollo Creed have felt to enter a ring with no opponent? No doubt he worked long and hard to prepare in anticipation of a fight. Had Apollo surrendered after the first round, he would have inevitably lost the battle. That is certainly one way to look at it. On the other hand, if Apollo had surrendered, he would have won the war for his life. The world celebrated Apollo's efforts as heroic. His fight provided inspiration for Rocky to take on the Russian himself. He was honored magnificently in the world of boxing and went down in the history books as one of the greatest fighters to have ever lived. Despite these accolades and recognition, Apollo lost simply because he was unwilling to surrender. He fought a battle that he could not win, even continuing beyond a vital warning. The price he paid was his life, but the aftermath of his decision survived to devastate those whom he loved. As far as what can be inferred from the actual movie scene, Apollo left a wife with a broken heart and two close friends in Rocky and his trainer, Duke. Your refusal to surrender to your imperfection is your fight and yours alone, but it is far from personal.

Now is the time to consider the affect your relentless pursuit of perfection might have on those you love most. We've already established the notion that your pursuit of perfection is selfish. We agree that the journey is altogether self-centered, leaving no room for intervention. Now I want you to imagine the trajectory of the lives of your family and friends without you in the picture. Sound a bit extreme? Maybe, but I cannot stress enough how potentially devastating your inability to surrender can be. Your spouse, your children, your parents, your brothers, and your sisters have never expected perfection of you or from you. At my weakest physical point when my body was ravished by my disease, my parents pleaded with me to proceed with the surgery. How could I have been so selfish, so blind to the concerns of my loved ones? Looking back, I can tell you precisely why. I still believed in my twisted mind that I could recover, and that kept my potential for perfection alive. I was as likely to survive my disease without surgery as Apollo Creed was of defeating the Russian. Pain, frustration, and disappointment are tremendously helpful if recognized and heeded before it's too late. Your life is not your own, and your pursuit of perfection will wreak havoc on those you hold closest. I realize now that I caused an entire life's worth of agony for my family as I fought my disease and my doctors. Herein lies the value of afterthought, and it is all so plain to see now. Had I known then that life on the other side of surrender could be so sweet, I would have volunteered for surgery; I would have been willing to gamble with my life. Take it from me; surrender the fight now and save your loved ones the heartache. You cannot win.

Surrender is not defeat but rather a step on the path of purpose. Up to this point in the chapter I have shared consequences of the failure to surrender. Maybe I'm applying scare tactics—I don't know! In case you're still not convinced, let me direct your attention to a few valiant displays of intestinal fortitude through surrender. I want to remind you that my intent is not to encourage defeat on any level but to open your mind to a much bigger picture. The goal of life is not perfection, and any effort to prove otherwise will end in defeat. It is my hope that you will see the value of surrender as a setup and not a setback through the lives of the following individuals. Each understood that surrender was necessary for a greater good.

At the top of the list is General Robert E. Lee, who was perhaps the most iconic and most widely respected of all Civil War commanders. Though he opposed secession, he resigned from the US Army to join the forces of his native state, rose to command the largest Confederate army, and ultimately was named general in chief of all Confederate land forces. He repeatedly defeated larger Federal armies in Virginia, but his two invasions of Northern soil were unsuccessful. In Ulysses S. Grant, he found an opponent who would not withdraw regardless of setbacks and casualties, and Lee's outnumbered forces were gradually reduced in number and forced into defensive positions that did not allow him room to maneuver. When he surrendered the Army of Northern Virginia at Appomattox Court House on April 9, 1865, it meant the war was virtually over. After the war, Lee and his family lived in Richmond until he accepted a position as president of Washington College (later renamed Washington and Lee University) in Lexington, Virginia, later in 1865.[6] On October 2, 1870, the heart disease that had plagued him for at least seven years finally claimed the old warrior. He had become a symbol of Southern resistance to the Union armies and was made an icon of the Lost Cause in the postwar South. Today he remains internationally respected as a daring, often brilliant tactician, a gentleman who never referred to Northern soldiers as "the enemy" but as "those people over there," a man who opposed secession but felt honor-bound to serve his native state. He applied for restoration of his American citizenship, but the papers were lost until the 1970s when his wish was granted. In the moment I am certain that Lee would have liked to have been anywhere other than sitting in front of Grant, offering his surrender. However, this incredible act of courage was nothing more than a temporary setback that set up the restoration of the United States and departure from war.

When I think of successful surrender, Jackie Robinson also comes to mind. Jack Roosevelt Robinson was born in Cairo, Georgia, in 1919 to a family of sharecroppers. His mother, Mallie Robinson, single-handedly raised Jackie and her four other children. They were the only black family on their block, and the prejudice they encountered only strengthened their bond. From this humble beginning would grow the first baseball player to break major league baseball's color barrier, which had segregated the sport for more than fifty years. In

---

6 http://www.historynet.com/robert-e-lee

1945, Jackie played one season in the Negro Baseball League, traveling all over the Midwest with the Kansas City Monarchs. But greater challenges and achievements were in store for him. In 1947, Brooklyn Dodgers president, Branch Rickey, approached Jackie about joining the Brooklyn Dodgers. The major leagues had not had an African-American player since 1889, when baseball became segregated. When Jackie first donned a Brooklyn Dodger uniform, he pioneered the integration of professional athletics in America. By breaking the color barrier in baseball, the nation's preeminent sport, he courageously challenged the deeply rooted custom of racial segregation in both the North and the South. Jackie Robinson's life and legacy will be remembered as one of the most important in American history.[7] In 1997, the world celebrated the fiftieth anniversary of Jackie's breaking major league baseball's color barrier. In doing so, we honored the man who stood defiantly against those who would work against racial equality and acknowledged the profound influence of one man's life on the American culture. Jackie Robinson surrendered his pride. He experienced extreme ridicule and was the subject of scorn for so long. This incredible act of surrender paved the way for African-American athletes to shine in sports of every kind.

And who could forget Lance Armstrong? I know his story has recently been revealed, thus unleashing a major controversy. Whether or not Lance Armstrong engaged in doping and should have been stripped of multiple Tour de France victories, the guy beat cancer through surrender. Armstrong surrendered to the reality that he must leave the sport he loved to pursue surgery and recovery so that he could survive. I have much respect for this guy for the comeback he so bravely made. Lance Armstrong's body was literally ravished before him. His testicular cancer diagnosis and subsequent surgery happened within a matter of moments. The body he worked so hard to build was destroyed by cancer; he could have easily rolled over and played victim. On the other hand, he could have allowed the cancer to overtake him and claim his life.

---

7 http://www.jackierobinson.com/about/bio.html

Allow me to present a side of Armstrong you might not have considered. Born on September 18, 1971, in Plano, Texas, Lance Armstrong was raised by his mother, Linda, in the suburbs of Dallas. Armstrong was athletic from an early age. He began running and swimming at ten years old, and he took up competitive cycling and triathlons (which combine a thousand-meter swim, fifteen-mile bike ride, and three-mile run) at thirteen. At sixteen Armstrong became a professional triathlete. He was the national sprint-course triathlon champion in 1989 and 1990. Soon Armstrong chose to focus on cycling, his strongest event as well as his favorite. During his senior year in high school the US Olympic development team invited him to train with them in Colorado Springs, Colorado. He left high school temporarily to do so, but later took private classes and received his high school diploma in 1989. The following summer he qualified for the 1990 junior world team and placed eleventh in the World Championship Road Race with the best time of any American since 1976. That same year he became the US national amateur champion and beat out many professional cyclists to win two major races, the First Union Grand Prix and the Thrift Drug Classic. In 1991, Armstrong competed in his first Tour DuPont, a long and difficult twelve-stage race covering 1,085 miles over eleven days. Though he finished in the middle of the pack, his performance announced a promising newcomer to the world of international cycling. He went on to win another stage race, the Settimana Bergamasca race, in Italy later that summer. After he finished second in the US Olympic time trials in 1992, Armstrong was favored to win the road race in Barcelona, Spain. With a surprisingly sluggish performance, however, he came in fourteenth.[8]

Undeterred, Armstrong turned professional immediately after the Olympics, joining the Motorola cycling team for a respectable yearly salary. Though he came in dead last in his first professional event, the day-long San Sebastian Classic in Spain, he rebounded in two weeks and

---

8 http://www.biography.com/people/lance-armstrong-9188901#related-video-gallery

finished second in a World Cup race in Zurich, Switzerland. Armstrong had a strong year in 1993, winning cycling's Triple Crown. Armstrong turned professional immediately, and the CoreStates Race (the US professional championship). That same year he came in second at the Tour DuPont. He started off well in his first Tour de France, a twenty-one-stage race that is widely considered cycling's most prestigious event. Though he won the eighth stage of the race, he later fell to sixty-second place and eventually pulled out. In August 1993, the twenty-one-year-old Armstrong won his most important race yet, the World Road Race Championship in Oslo, Norway, a one-day event covering 161 miles. As the leader of the Motorola team, he overcame difficult conditions—pouring rain made the roads slick and caused him to crash twice during the race—to become the youngest person and only second American ever to win that contest.

Leading up to his diagnosis in October 1996, Armstrong had been training and racing as a professional triathlete and cyclist for four years. Predating the launch of his professional career was fifteen years of swimming, cycling, and running. The guy was dedicated beyond imagination and lived for his sport. The cancer could not have come at a more inconvenient time, yet he accepted it and began his comeback first by surrender. The initial surgery was successful, but Armstrong had a long road ahead. All the while he maintained his focus and determination. He surrendered any bitterness and resentment and poured that energy into his recovery. Lance Armstrong made his comeback sixteen months removed from his two surgeries in February 2007. He brought his body back gradually. Forty-five-minute rides became two-hour rides, which became hundred-mile training rides. Over time, his muscles reappeared and he rediscovered his engine. By January 2008, he was among the strongest riders in training camp on a strong US Postal Service team. Armstrong will forever be in the record books for mounting a comeback of epic proportions. At the beginning of his comeback was a temporary setback. I think you know what I'm going to say, *but* ... surrender! Love him or hate him, it is very hard to dispute the global good of his Livestrong Foundation. Armstrong established the foundation in

1997 as a way to raise awareness. Today the organization looks for new ways to raise awareness, increase outreach, and facilitate collaboration in an effort to improve the cancer experience. Since our inception, the foundation has raised more than $500 million dollars for the fight against cancer, with 82 percent of those funds going directly to support programs and services for survivors.

At the core of surrender is change, and that's not something we like to chew on. Change is one of life's greatest blessings, but it comes in disguise. As the late Joseph Campbell has said, "We must let go of the life we have planned so as to accept the one that is waiting for us." I often wonder why I still struggle so much with change. It was change that saved my life. It was change that led me to my passion (which I will discuss in detail in the chapters to come). I am a living, breathing example of the benefits of change, yet I continue to struggle. We may have tried once to pursue our passion; however, things did not go as planned and we got burned. So we built walls of certainty designed to protect against the unknown. We would rather be mediocre than uncertain.

Surrendering to perfection is not settling for mediocrity, but there will be peaks and valleys. The willingness to surrender through change is essential for the setup you so desperately seek. Don't get me wrong. It's fine to dream of the life you desire to live, but don't stop there. Do something about it! In fact, the first thing you can do is surrender to the inevitable change that has been taunting you for so long. Nothing in life lasts forever. Change happens and can be the difference in thriving and merely surviving. The majority of people in the world today are creatures of habit. We are attracted to what is familiar and establish routines to protect against uncertainty. We seek personal comfort and avoid anything that could potentially interrupt the status quo. The problem with this mind-set is that it can easily lead to mediocrity and obscurity. We rob ourselves of potential greatness because of our fear of the unknown. We do what is necessary to get by rather than taking chances that could lead to breakthroughs. Unfortunately we cannot change the fact that our lives will change. The opportunity comes with our perception of and reaction to change. It is not a temporary convenience but a blessing in disguise. If we could bring ourselves to see beyond the initial inconvenience and focus on the possibilities, the trajectory of most of our lives would be drastically different. That ability comes through faith. That's right. The best version of you waits on the other side of change. I could not find a more appropriate quote to further illustrate this point than William Coffin's words, "I love the recklessness of faith. First you leap, and then you grow wings."

Surrender is the strongest step you can take up to this point in your struggle with perfection. You will only surrender when you're ready. No matter how much evidence I present, despite the fact that I'm alive today to share my experience, it's all for naught if you have not yet reached the point of readiness. The remainder of this story is extremely practical. I've made a strong case to help you identify the imperfection in your life, but now it's time to point you in the direction of correction! If you still feel that perfection is possible, I simply ask that you put down this book and return when you experience the heartache, failure, and disappointment that your current path will surely bring you. I hope with all my heart that you are ready to join me now on the path to purpose, which will never be perfect!

CHAPTER 3

Potential Points the Way

The potential of the average person is like a huge ocean unsailed,
a new continent unexplored, a world of possibilities waiting to be
released and channeled toward some great good.

—Brian Tracy

I cannot imagine a more dismal ending than to die with potential. The name itself implies wasted talent. Potential is the foundation. Potential is the launch pad for an abundant life, but possibility and capability are *not* activities. To make it through life with unrealized potential is a life largely devoid of meaning and significance. With that in mind, let me ask you a question. Are you uncomfortable yet? At this point you have either surrendered your pursuit of perfection or have come to the realization that it is indeed your next step. Congratulations! You are now well on your way to finding your purpose in life. Surrender is a temporary setback, I assure you. Although temporary, it does ensure immediate relief. You are most likely anxious at this point. You have finally reached the point where you realize you are not in control. You can now see that the perfect version of you just doesn't exist. I say again congratulations! After all, you are a human being! Your surrender is so sweet, and you now understand and accept that your perfection will never be. You have successfully surrendered to a battle that has no meaning or purpose. Perfection is impossible, but purpose is not, so let's get on with it.

The path to purpose starts with surrender. That much we've determined. Now we must shift our focus from what is to what could (and should) be. For the purpose of this illustration your imperfection exists, but you still have potential. What would you do if time or money were of no concern? If you had twenty-five hours in a day and a million dollars in the bank, how would you approach the day? What do you enjoy doing above all else? What are you good at? What do others say that you do best? Let your mind go to that place where you are most at ease. Your talents and interests serve as the foundation for your potential. Surrender paves the way for your potential to perform. Like purpose, potential is not perfect. Potential is the first step in the right direction toward purpose and away from perfection. Wherever you are at this point in life, you have the potential to move. Your first inclination may or may not be right, but you're okay with that because you've surrendered.

This step on the purpose process is rooted in self-awareness. This is your potential in question. This is how you perceive your place in the world and not how the world sees you. Either you establish your potential by identifying talent and making a conscious effort to move toward it, or the world will do it for you through the expectations of others. If you ever hope to discover your purpose in life, you have to be the one calling the shots in the early stages. If you pursue your interests and develop talent for the approval of others, you will never find your purpose. You were created as a unique being unlike any other on the face of the earth. Your purpose is out there for you and you alone to find. I'm not saying that you shouldn't be influenced, but ultimately you must be the one to make the decision.

Your potential is where talent and interest collide. Interests are the result of what you do, what you learn, and the people you know. These factors change year to year as your knowledge and experience grow. Talents are the result of inheritance and early development. Interests are certainly influenced by outside forces whereas talents usually are not. You can certainly have one without the other, but the result will never be potential. Let me try to explain with an illustration from my own life. I grew up in a family of golfers. My dad played golf. My grandparents as well as most of my friends also played. Naturally I gravitated toward the game of golf, but did I love it? Not exactly, but I didn't dislike it either. I played competitively through high school and even tried to play in college. All the while I felt as if I was doing it for my family. Golf was both an interest and somewhat of a talent for me as a kid; however, it was not indicative of my purpose, and I did not stick with it. I think most of us are influenced from an early age toward a particular path to a certain extent. Let's stick with golf for the following consideration. Tiger Woods, who is now considered one of the greatest players to have ever lived, first appeared on the *Johnny Carson Show* with a putter at the age of two. Clearly this was a result of his father's influence. When Tiger came along, Earl Woods was determined that his son start golf early. Taking him to the Navy Golf Course, which was just five minutes from their home, Earl put a putter into Tiger's hands before he could walk and taught him the fundamentals of the game before he could barely talk. Earl poured himself into his young son, and it wasn't long until Tiger hit his stride. By the age of three he'd already scored fifty on nine holes and outputted Bob Hope on the *Mike Douglas Show*. Still, if observers needed further proof that Woods was a child prodigy, they got it when he hit a hole-in-one at the age of six and broke eighty by the age of eight. However, Tiger's talent was not limited to golf. During his teen years he participated in many sports. *Newsweek* acknowledged that Woods was "a natural switch-hitter" [in baseball], loved playing shooting guard [in basketball], was a wide receiver [in football], and a 400-meter runner [in track]. But golf always seemed to be his main love, so much so that his parents often had to remind or encourage him to do other things. Not only was Tiger extremely talented at a very young age, but he also had a work ethic that rivaled men three times his age.[9] (There is more to come on the power of pursuit in the next chapter, which marks the next step on the purpose process.) The difference between my early experience as a golfer and Tiger Woods is that Tiger loved the game—and the rest is history!

---

9 http://www.encyclopedia.com/topic/Tiger_Woods.aspx

Let's consider the opposite side of the picture—interest without talent. You don't have to look far to run into this painful reality. *American Idol* anyone? I cannot think of a more despicable display of mediocrity! There are the extraordinary exceptions, but for the most part the primary drivers of TV ratings are those who think they can sing. The saving grace of this scenario is that talent is more easily developed. I have no singing ability whatsoever, but let's just say I had the desire to learn. Coaching ability is essential for the development of talent. If I put forth the time and energy, I am confident I could learn to sing and actually sound tolerable. My point is that talent can be coached. However, interest cannot. As the saying goes, "Desire cannot be taught, it must be caught." My personal take on this alliteration is to simply find those daring souls with determined desire built in!

Talent and interest are closely related yet vastly different. You are certainly aware of your interests, but your talents are often more apparent through the observation of those around you. You may think you have talent in a particular area, but the only way to know for sure is to engage others who come into contact with your perceived talent. Consider your current working environment. Do you feel that your talents are being fully utilized? More importantly, are you interested in the details of your work? Remember, we are trying to identify potential, which we agreed is the intersection of your talent and interest. Either you are engaged and challenged by your work or you are not. How did you choose your vocation to begin with? Why did you decide to pursue the course of study you chose? Did your decision come from a point of interest or talent? Ideally your interest was higher in the beginning; however, your talent has now caught up and the result is full engagement. Potential is only the first step on your path to purpose, so please don't lose heart. There is nothing wrong with discontentment as long as it leads to action. You may enjoy certain aspects of your work and lack ability, or you may rock in terms of proficiency but have no interest in the substance of the work itself. Whatever camp you fall into, the most important matter is that you recognize it and take steps to remedy it.

Start by asking anyone in your immediate environment, "What am

I good at? What are my weaknesses?" Let me warn you on the front end. Do not ask if you are not ready to listen to the voice of reason! Or in other words, in this case ignorance is most certainly not bliss! This simple question is incredibly powerful and can open your mind to a world otherwise unnoticed. If you are genuinely interested in seeking feedback, I think it can work wonders. Feedback is essential because you are not in observation of your actions twenty-four hours per day. It would be different if somehow you discovered a way to operate with a mirror projecting a 360 degree view of your being! How do you know if you possess a certain talent that benefits others? How do you know if your interests are similar to those of others around you? It's simple. You ask and listen! You may have an idea of where you think you should go, but what if an alternate path resulted in a greater good for a larger group of people? For example, we've all heard the derogatory phrase, "Those who cannot do, teach [or coach]." I have a major issue with this statement. Additionally, the best players do not always make the best coaches or the top producers the best managers. What if a player or producer had a greater talent for coaching but were never made aware of it by those in their environment? A player may have plenty of talent on the field or court but could have a much greater gifting for the sidelines. My point is that unless you seek and listen, you might be living a lesser calling for your life. This is where the observations of your closest friends and family members can do you a world of good!

Okay, these are all hypotheticals designed to set your mind toward the things you enjoy. Chances are if interest precedes talent, you are operating at full potential. As we surmised earlier, talent can be coached, but desire cannot, so if you are good at something but do not enjoy it, what's the point? Let's walk through a practical exercise that you can immediately apply to your life. The goal is to reach the realization that you are either living out your potential or not. I want you to give serious thought to the following questions before you answer:

1) What do your parents do for a living?
2) Do you have brother and sisters, or are you an only child?

3) Can you remember a particular teacher in elementary or high school who had a tremendous impact on your life?
4) Were you exposed to athletics or music at an early age?
5) Were you a socialite or loner as a child?
6) Was your family in the habit of taking regular vacations where you were exposed to different parts of the world?
7) If you attended college, what criteria were most crucial in making your decision?
8) Why it is that you chose the vocation in which you currently serve?
9) Do you love what you do, or is it a means to an end?
10) Are you engaged in any recreational activities outside of your work environment?
11) What do you dream about?

Why do you enjoy the things you do, and where did your talent come from? Some would argue that talent is born. Still others feel that talent is developed. I guess either side of this argument works. This series of self-reflective questions is designed to help you arrive at the origin of your unique created being. Let's consider each and go a bit deeper. If you grew up in a home with one or both parents, chances are the work that was done in front of you motivated you. Either you were positively influenced toward the same profession or you were motivated to do whatever possible to avoid that path. The size of your family also is an influential factor on your potential. If you had a large family, there were certainly more children to care for, and so you might have received less attention. On the other hand, if you were the only child, you might have a tendency toward control. Outside of your home, were there any other adults you can remember as significant in your development? If so, I'll bet that you can remember details about those people. I am going to go out on a limb here and guess that some of your best qualities today are a result of the time and energy this person poured into you! Did you first reach for a ball or a bell? If you are athletic, you probably remember the person who first played catch with you. If, on the other hand, you are a musical whiz, I am sure you remember the one who first taught you how to read music.

As far as social interactions went, were you the life of the party or the one standing in the corner? One is not better than the other, but your demeanor is a reflection of your upbringing. Do you live with an open mind and sense of adventure, or do you prefer to keep to the familiar? Again, one is not better than the other. This is simply an exercise for you to reflect on in order to arrive at a logical determination of whether or not you are living your potential. Did you leave home and attend college in another state, or did you stick close to home or forgo college altogether? Have you thought about why you first chose the work that you are performing now? While I'm on the subject, are you pleased with the path you are walking? Do you love your work and live for it day in and day out, or do you do it just to live?

Thus far I have been largely impartial on these potential responses, but this is one that I have a strong feeling for. In today's world you really have no excuse for working a job you do not love. We live in the age of technology. The Internet has completely leveled the playing field. If you do not currently love what you do, the workplace is ripe for your very own creation. That's right. If you can't find your dream job, build it! In case you are wondering about my logic, take a look at Facebook, Twitter, Amazon, and Apple! I do feel it is extremely beneficial to love your work. (After all, you give the majority of your waking hours to this place.) Likewise, a robust extracurricular life will add to the building of your character. Sports, music, travel, wine-tasting, gardening—just pick something and allow yourself to drift toward it on a regular basis. Work without play is no way to spend the day!

Finally, let me ask a personal question. Do you dream? Or better yet, do you dare to dream beyond the images that occur in your subconscious when your head is on the pillow? Is there a gap between where you are now and where you would like to be? Why is that? What have you not done (yet) to close that gap? The gap is your dream and the closure is discipline and desire. Remember those famous words of Walt Disney, "If you can dream it, you can do it." If you really want to develop your potential, you will find a way. If you do not, you'll find an excuse.

Another popular way to determine your potential is through aptitude testing. Aptitude tests are systematic ways of evaluating how people perform in tasks or react to different situations. They have standardized methods of administration and scoring and the results are compared with how others have done on the same tests. Aptitude testing will have much more to do with your talents than interests, but if you've already conducted a personal assessment as well as surveyed those to whom you are closest in life, this is a fantastic next step. There are hundreds of aptitude tests available today ranging from free, do-it-yourself versions to highly organized, professional services-type tests. The ones that I'm most familiar with are the DISC assessment, the Meyers-Briggs, and the Johnson O'Conner.

DISC is a personal assessment tool used to improve work productivity, teamwork, and communication. The initial DISC model comes from Dr. William Marston, a professor at Columbia University in the 1920s who was curious about the behavior of normal people.[10] He did not create an instrument from his theory, but others did. If you participate in a DISC program, you'll be asked to complete a series of questions that produce a detailed report about your personality and behavior. The DISC model provides a common language people can use to better understand themselves and to adapt their behaviors with others. This can be done within a work team, a sales relationship, a leadership position, or other relationships. DISC profiles help you and your team:

- increase your self-knowledge (i.e., how you respond to conflict, what motivates you, what causes you stress, and how you solve problems),
- facilitate better teamwork and minimize team conflict,

---

10 https://www.discprofile.com/what-is-disc/overview/

- develop stronger sales skills by identifying and responding to customer styles,
- manage more effectively by understanding the dispositions and priorities of employees and team members, and
- become more self-knowledgeable, well-rounded, and effective leaders.

The letters stand for dominance, influence, steadiness, and conscientiousness. A dominant person places emphasis on accomplishing results and the bottom line, and he or she is quite confident. An influential person places emphasis on influencing or persuading others and fostering openness; this individual is a great relationship builder. A steady person places emphasis on cooperation and sincerity, and he or she is highly dependable. Lastly, the conscientiousness person places emphasis on quality, accuracy, and expertise, valuing competency. If this particular route sounds attractive, you can learn more about the enrollment process at https://www.discprofile.com/resources-and-tools/faq/.

The Meyers-Briggs instrument (MBTI) has been used for more than fifty years and it is continually updated through ongoing research to improve its ability to meaningfully identify character traits. The most recent update included the use of a representative national sample. No other personality test is backed by as much research and as many years of use as is the MBTI instrument, which has been taken by millions of people worldwide. The MBTI assessment was the first tool to describe healthy, normal personalities rather than abnormal ones. It identifies sixteen personality types that are each equally valid and healthy. Knowledge of psychological type helps people better understand themselves and one another, resulting in more effective and satisfying human achievement. An advantage of the MBTI assessment is that knowing your personality type will help you understand yourself and your behaviors better. Knowing your type may also help you appreciate others' styles and thus enable you to use differences more constructively. You will gain a greater understanding of your strengths, enabling yourself to look for opportunities to use those strengths for more effective functioning in work and life.[11] For the purpose of this inclusion, strengths would refer to your talents. The MBTI instrument has four sets of letters:

- "E" and "I" stand for extraversion and introversion, indicating whether you receive energy from being around people or from time spent alone.
- "S" and "N" stand for sensing and intuition, indicating whether you become aware of specific facts and concrete details or prefer to focus on hunches and the big picture.
- "T" and "F" stand for thinking and feeling, indicating whether you tend to make decisions based on logical analysis and the principles involved or prefer to decide by considering your values and promoting harmony for the people involved.
- "J" and "P" stand for judging and perceiving, indicating whether you prefer your life to be planned and like it when things are decided or you prefer to go with the flow and like keeping your options open.

If this is the test for you, you can access the enrollment at https://www. mbticomplete.com/en/Register.aspx.

Last but not least is the Johnson O'Conner aptitude assessment. This is the one I have personal experience with, so naturally I'm a bit biased. There's a funny story about my introduction to this test. My wife's grandparents insisted that she and her four siblings undergo this particular test (along with all the other grandchildren in a family with five siblings). I never heard the story on how the grandparents developed their loyalty to Johnson O'Conner, but nonetheless, I was heavily influenced by their wishes. Early on in our marriage when we were gathered together with our extended family, the subject of Johnson O'Conner would consistently surface. Finally my curiosity got the best

---

11 https://www.mbticomplete.com/contents/Faq.aspx#faq23

of me and I asked my wife's grandfather why he felt so strongly about this test. What I heard was enough to convince me to take the test myself In the spring of 2009, I drove to Atlanta, Georgia, to the closest Johnson O'Conner testing facility in my area. For the record, I detest standardized examinations so I was not all thrilled with the testing environment. Much to my delight and surprise, my perception was not consistent with reality. The instructor started with a conversation and then asked me to perform a series of exercises. I would later learn that a key point of differentiation with Johnson O'Conner was that the tests did not consist of answering questions or filling out forms. Johnson O'Conner felt that it was too easy to answer a question depending on mood or opinion. Even if approached sincerely, a personality test or interest questionnaire's results were based solely on how the subjects felt about themselves, not on ability for a particular task. According to Johnson O'Conner, your natural abilities (aptitudes) come to you from your parents or grandparents and not from learning. You cannot change your natural aptitudes any more than you can change your eye color. A larger amount of knowledge generally will help you be more successful in whatever you are doing, but a larger number of aptitudes may prove to be detrimental. Furthermore, Johnson O'Conner believes that unused aptitudes not only go to waste but often cause unrest and distraction. An inventory of aptitudes is not intended to select the one and only career path for you, but if you know your abilities, you will be able to follow certain principles in making choices at each decision point during your life.[12]

Enter the guinea pig—me! The test reveals a combination of aptitudes uncovered in the testing process. These abilities are then paired with career paths as suggestions. Aptitude testing is a very effective tool for educational and career selection in that it provides an unbiased, factual representation of how you think and work. With that in mind, my test results suggested work of an individual nature. My personality type was scored as subjective and is characteristic of those

---

12 https://www.jocrf.org

in the specialized professions, such as consultant, journalist, teacher, or small specialty business owner. I was also tagged with *ideaphoria,* the ability to generate a rapid flow of ideas that can be used to inform and educate others. At the time of my test I served as a financial advisor and managed the personal retirement portfolios of 150 families. My scores seemed pretty accurate at the time, but they are now even more so. Last year I transitioned my position in the world of investment management from advisor for individuals to consultant for advisors. I had a fantastic experience with Johnson O'Conner and recommend it highly. If you are at all curious as to whether or not you would be a good candidate for testing at this point in your life, consider the following profile description as stated on the Johnson O'Conner website:

> About half our clients are employed adults who want help in planning their career path. Adults who decide to take advantage of the Foundation's aptitude testing program include people unhappy or dissatisfied by their current jobs, those facing promotions or transfers, and those who are facing downsizing or other types of career transition. It is also valuable for adults considering further education, contemplating opening a business, who are thinking about entirely new careers, or who are returning to work after raising a family. Even those about to retire who are looking for ways to make their retirement years satisfying and productive may find that learning about their aptitudes helps them make more informed decisions.[13]

Potential is the first stop on the way to purpose. Just as a dog was created to bark and a kangaroo to jump, you were created for a unique purpose unlike any other, and I simply suggest a course of action to help you find it. I found my purpose but it took twenty-six years, so I'd like to save you time if at all possible. As human beings, we were created to thrive and not merely survive. We celebrate those who found their

---

13 http://www.jocrf.org/about_aptitudes/who.html

potential and developed it. After all, the world is better off because of it. Just imagine what life would be like if Henry Ford never mastered the art of innovation, thus revolutionizing the automobile industry in the early twentieth century. Or for that matter, what would the world of computing be without Bill Gates and Steve Jobs? These three men lived out their unique purposes and created masterpieces along the way. To thrive is to discover your potential as early as possible and develop it to the fullest extent. (There's more to come on this pursuit in the chapters to follow.) To thrive is to experience victory, but survival is simply doing enough to get by. As I stated earlier, I believe my life was spared to share this message. I can honestly say that for the first twenty-six years of my life, I would have rather been dead. I had a classic case of "stinkin' thinkin.'" I played the victim. In the time since my life-saving surgery, I have walked the process that serves as the subject of this book. Now I know we are only on the first step, but I have goose bumps thinking about your response at the end. Potential paves the way, but we're just getting started!

CHAPTER 4

Plan with a Pivot

You can't plan life. Because no matter how perfect your plan is, life has a way to rearrange it.

—Mina Deanna

I can't exactly say I saw this one coming. At the very moment I write these words, I am recounting a dramatic change of plans that nearly derailed this entire book project. You already know this book has been a work long in the making, but this week in particular was an incredible inconvenience that I just had to roll with. I was in Atlanta on business that required two nights in a hotel. I arrived late on a Tuesday afternoon, checked in, and then ventured out to see what I could find for dinner. I found a great spot nearby and placed my order. I walked down to a coffee shop and caught up on some e-mails as I waited for my dinner. Thirty minutes later I was back in my car headed for the hotel with dinner and visions of a sound night's sleep I ate dinner, read a little bit, and then hit the hay. I slept very well and was up at 5:00 a.m. to begin the day. As I walked to my car under the darkness of the early morning, I noticed that something was out of place. As I got closer my heart sank and my eyes took in the sickening sight. *I had been robbed.* What else can I say other than I felt completely violated and helpless? My mind was racing as I regained my faculties. I began to assess the damage and determine exactly what had been stolen. The window behind my driver's side door had been shattered, but my suit was still hanging in the place I had left it the night before. I felt a bit of relief begin to settle in, but as I looked deeper inside the car, I could see that my briefcase had been stolen. I looked inside the driver's side door and found my wallet securely in place as well as my cell phone tucked away in the console where I had left it. I couldn't imagine what this thief was thinking, but my thoughts returned to my briefcase. My laptop (on which I was writing this manuscript), iPad, numerous chargers, and presentation accessories were all gone. This is when I started to panic. I had twenty thousand words written and stored on my laptop and I wasn't about to start over. What was I going to do? I certainly didn't plan for this to happen, but that did not take away that *it still happened.*

I had executed my plan without a hitch. I had written twelve straight days and was leaps and bounds ahead of my deadline. Up to this point my plan included sixty-nine days of writing with six-hundred-word goals each day. There was nothing in my plan that included a burglary. Now, looking back on this fateful day I can honestly say I'm glad it happened. How in good conscience can I write a book about change management and flexibility if I myself come unglued when my plan doesn't work out exactly as I thought? As a matter of fact, my unfortunate incident in Atlanta only increased my conviction in this message. Life does not go according to plan. There are always variables we cannot account for. Sure, I was upset and put out for a temporary period of time. I had to go through the hassle of filing a police report and a claim with my insurance company. I had to pay a deductible for the replacement property and drive four hours on the interstate with a missing window on a hot summer day. These details come with the territory, but ultimately I recovered and gained even more resilience than I'd had when I had started the project. It's going to take far more than a burglary to keep me from casting this vision!

Hopefully by now you've accepted the fact that perfection is impossible. That doesn't mean you have to accept a lesser version of yourself or that you still cannot find your purpose, but your life won't be perfect! So why do we continue to plan without margin? We spent the previous chapter on potential and defined it as the gap between where you are now and where you want to be. Potential is worthless unless acted upon. Now is the time when we turn to application, and the first stop on this route is your plan. Don't go too crazy at the onset. After all, you need to stay in this if you ever hope to develop potential. Your plan will move your thoughts into action. The world is full of brilliant thinkers but few daring innovators. Who knows, your plan could be exactly what the world needs to spin a little faster. (Chances are it won't, but you need to pep yourself up to move, which is largely counterintuitive.) My primary intent with this chapter is to open your mind to a concept I call "pivot planning." Humor me with my basketball terminology, but the inference is made to identify the necessity of dynamic planning. Come on. When's the last time your plan worked exactly as you expected? Just as there is no such thing as the perfect life, a perfect plan is a fairy tale.

Let's pick apart the principle of the perfect plan. It starts with you at the center with an idea of how to develop your potential. First you visualize your current surroundings and are haunted by feelings of disgust. You quickly move your thoughts to the place where you feel most alive. I guess some would call this daydreaming. If you're an employee of a Fortune 500 company, you may dream about owning your own business. Perhaps you have political aspirations with visions of one day holding a seat in the House of Representatives. In order for your dream to become a reality you have to plot your path. So you go to work, furiously recording every minute detail that will lead you to your happy place. It is precisely in this moment that you (perhaps unknowingly) plan for perfection. You tell yourself, "How could something that feels so right be wrong in any way?" The plan has been established and you are committed to it. The problem with this is that the world doesn't work that way. Believe it or not, you are not the only human being on the face of the earth! Let's say you're the brand new business owner. In order to hire your first employee, you need a loan right away. Never mind your personal banker is out sick the day you visit or that his replacement requests more background information than you are used to providing.

The ebbs and flows of everyday life swing quite differently depending on the matter and the particular circumstances. Your personal bankers certainly did not intend to be sick on the day you needed him most. He had no way of knowing you needed the loan so expeditiously. Accidents, mistakes, coincidences, luck, fate—these things happen, so why would you not account for them as you plan your potential?

Do you consider yourself a strategic person? Do you plan out of habit, or do you avoid the practice at any cost? I love the scene in the movie *Along Came Polly* when Ben Stiller and Jennifer Aniston are stuck in the bow of ship during a terrifying storm. The context of their conversation is long-term planning. Stiller plays a risk-assessment analyst who is paid to plan life down to the very detail. Quite the opposite, Aniston plays a carefree, fly-by-the-seat-of-her-pants artist. Their lives could not be any more different. During this particular scene Stiller is arguing the case that Aniston has no plan for her future by saying, "You're on the non-plan plan." Aniston responds, "I am not on the non-plan plan!" thus ending the argument. This exchange is a wonderful example of two completely different personality types. If you've seen the movie, you know that Stiller plays a neurotic perfectionist while Aniston more or less takes things as they come. This movie represents both ends of the spectrum, but I think if you have hope of taking that first step toward finding your potential, you would be better served to adopt Aniston's outlook.

There is no disputing that planning is a necessity of life. Plans exist to keep us from killing one another and to coexist somewhat peacefully in a world that gets more chaotic by the minute! Undoubtedly we've all heard the age-old saying, "If you fail to plan, you are planning to fail." There are hundreds, if not thousands, of books on the subject of strategic planning. Plans allow you to categorize and prioritize the thoughts swimming in your mind. Now, remember that a plan has two primary components—thoughts and actions. You are the creator of your thoughts, but actions are directed and redirected by outside forces at work. Let's revisit the aspiring politician to demonstrate. The thought is clear—public office. The actions necessary to convert the thought into reality are a bit more complicated. Because this thought is not a solo mission, other people will gain influence over the potential outcome. This is where the realization of imperfect planning becomes critical. Because we all exist as human beings we are prone to error, which has nothing to do with intentions. I found this quote from Norman MacDonald most appropriate: "Do not imagine that the good you intend will balance the evil you perform." By including others in your plan, you compromise ultimate control of your desired outcome.

Planning involves people, which can lead to problems. This is a natural part of life and certainly no excuse to paralyze your potential. It is important that you anticipate this notion so that you are not caught off guard *when* (not if) it happens. So what do you do when your plans suddenly fail? The fact that you had a plan to begin with is not enough to redirect responsibility. If the plan was indeed your own, your first step is to accept responsibility. The quickest way to alienate yourself from your team is to point the finger. A collective failure is a unique opportunity if you chose to see it as such. I think about the greatest inventions in the history of mankind and what was required. When asked by a reporter how he felt after he had failed so many times before he finally invented the lightbulb, Thomas Edison responded, "I have not failed. I've just found ten thousand ways that won't work." Don't you love that attitude? You do if you have any real hope of reaching your full potential. What Edison knew (along with Henry T. Ford, Alexander Graham Bell, Steve Jobs, and Bill Gates) was that failure was fantastic as long as it wasn't final. You know, the more I think about it, the more I wish I could have a conversation with Benjamin Franklin to convince him to rethink his famous quote. Rather than saying, "If you fail to plan, you plan to fail," he should have said, "If you don't plan to fail, you will fail your plan." Expect the unexpected, anticipate the audible, protect against being caught off guard, and you will have built for yourself a fortress from which to attack your plan!

Thank goodness life doesn't always go as we intend. If my life had gone according to plan, I am confident I would not be here today. I've shared that surgery was recommended far sooner than when I finally complied. Life according to me ended that fateful night in a Canadian emergency room. Looking back over the last eight years, I think about all the wonderful things I have experienced. Thank goodness life doesn't always go as planned! Perhaps you are down on your luck and just cannot seem to catch a break. If this is you and your life stinks, I hope you believe when I tell you I understand. For thirteen years I had a stomachache that would not go away. It was a daily ritual for me to visit the bathroom fifteen to twenty times. While my friends were playing sports and going to parties, I was lying flat on my back in anticipation of the next stomachache. I played the victim for far too long and lost the better part of my teenage and college years. None of that was part of the plan, but then again neither was the ruptured colon that left me fighting for my life. The life I lead today is a testimony to the necessity of pivotal planning.

Think of it like this. When plans go wrong, an opportunity for resiliency and adaptability rises to the surface. Dr. Martin Luther King, Jr., once said, "The ultimate measure of a man is not where he stands in moments of comfort and convenience, but where he stands at times of challenge and controversy." How would you define controversy? I'm inclined to place imperfect plans in that category, aren't you? This quote is the epitome of resilience and is precisely what is required to move through life's many challenges. We all know that life is far from perfect and ultimately we fall short. But then again the goal of life is not perfection. Not only should we not be surprised by hardship, but we should expect it. Adopting this mind-set will allow for a more flexible outlook on life. The world is not out to get you, although it may feel that way more days than not. The victim says, "Why me? Why now?" But the victor says, "Why not right now!" Think very carefully before you respond to this question. Which one are you?

I'd like to consider one of the greatest fighters of all time to further illustrate this point. Let's start with a quote from the infamous Mike Tyson: "Everybody has a plan until they get punched in the face." As controversial as Tyson has been over the years, there is tremendous value in this statement. Early in his career Tyson made a practice of destroying his opponents in the first round. He was a force to be reckoned with, a combination of raw power and speed. His plan was to attack early and often and not back down until his opponent was out. This strategy served him very well and is responsible for much of his early success. In 1988, at the age of twenty-two, Tyson defeated world champion Michael Spinks, a previously unbeaten boxing guru, after ninety-one seconds in the first round. That victory set the tone for the foreseeable future with Tyson winning nineteen of his first professional fights by knockout. Tyson's plan was going exactly as planned—that is, until February of 1990, when Tyson met his match in Buster Douglas. Going into the fight, Mike Tyson was the undefeated and undisputed heavyweight champion of the world. Despite his fair share of personal struggles, he was still a punisher in the ring and no doubt the overwhelming favorite. Tyson was viewed as such a dominant heavyweight that he was not only considered the world's top heavyweight but often the number-one fighter in the world pound for pound, a rarity for heavyweights. Buster Douglas was ranked as just the seventh best heavyweight by *Ring Magazine*, and he had met with mixed success in his professional boxing career up to that point.[14] From the beginning of the fight it was apparent that Douglas was not afraid. He displayed a lot of spring and life in his body movement, and he wasn't cautious in letting his punches fly whenever he saw the opportunity to attack Tyson. In the middle rounds Tyson managed to land a few of his signature uppercuts, but Douglas was still dominating the fight. In the tenth round Mike Tyson pushed forward to fight, but he was still seriously hurting from the accumulation of punishment given throughout the match. As Tyson walked forward, Douglas measured him with a few jabs before he landed a devastating uppercut that snapped Tyson's head upward, stopping Tyson in his tracks. As Tyson began to reel back from the uppercut, Douglas immediately followed with four punches to the head, knocking Tyson down for the first time in his career. Although it cannot

---

14 http://en.wikipedia.org/wiki/Mike_Tyson_vs._Buster_Douglas

be proven, I would guess Tyson uttered this famous quote precisely at the time he lost this fight.

So you've just been *punched*. Now what? I'm glad you asked. It's time to consider the pivot plan. For memory's sake I have framed this process with the acronym PLAN.

P: Ponder your potential.
L: Live your life.
A: Anticipate your anxiety.
N: Never mind your negativity.

This is a mind-set, a way of programming a new mental strategy. Thoughts without action are only theories and will get you nowhere. On the other hand, actions without thought are more often than not just reckless and only lead to trouble. Consider the concept of revenge, where motivation comes strictly from a desire to be vindicated. A primary action leads to a reaction, which results in damage. This is not an application of the pivot plan, and the goal is not to produce additional heartache. You have to start with an idea. No, wait! *You have to start with an action!* An idea is a given. You are now ready to do something with it. Don't bother putting together a plan if you never intend to pursue it. Intentions are worthless. We'll get into the mechanics of the pursuit in the next chapter, but at this point you have to know where your first step will take you.

Change is one of life's greatest blessings, but it most often comes in disguise. My life is an example of the wonders that change can bring, but you must first become comfortable with being uncomfortable. Interruptions, distractions, detours—these are all parts of life. Rather than becoming annoyed by these inconveniences, we should learn to expect them. Just as curveballs create opportunities for resilience, we should position distractions as setups for pivot planning. Think back to your last inconvenience and visualize your surroundings. To what single factor did you attribute your inconvenience? Why was it such a bother? Chances are it was this very thing that caused your plans to crumble.

It was most likely not a huge deal, but it was probably that you were simply not expecting it. When it happened, you allowed it to affect the rest of your day. Am I warm? This is where premeditated consideration can be so valuable. I suggest setting aside ten minutes at the beginning of each day to ponder the day ahead. Picture yourself going through the motions and go ahead and plan for distractions. If you are mentally prepared before the day begins, you will be more likely to operate on an even keel. Next, go ahead and let the day unfold as it will; you'll realize that most of the day is out of your immediate control anyway. Live your life with this reality and avoid the extremes. It will do wonders for your psyche.

Moving right along, you must be able to anticipate activity that will lead to anxiety. All human beings are prone to worry about something. It is important that you identify your triggers and anticipate the occurrence; this will eliminate the element of surprise that always intensifies your current emotions, good or bad. Lastly, if you can train your mind to refrain from negativity as a first response, you will be much more likely to accept and adapt. The pivot plan will allow you to maintain composure by anticipating anxiety and adjusting your attitude before the circumstances of life cause you to become unglued. If Mike Tyson could have anticipated the assault from Buster Douglas, perhaps he could have saved a bit of strength and salvaged the overall outcome of the fight. It is not enough to have a carefully thought-out plan; that much is under your complete control. You need a plan with the ability to pivot at the onset of surprise. Planning can feel like action, but it is really no different than talking. Until you actually do something (the context of the next chapter), you are no further along the path than when you started your plan.

It is crucial that you plan with a pencil and be open to any new direction life may bring. Case in point, consider my career as a financial advisor. I grew up watching my father pursue his career as stockbroker. He used to take me on client appointments and I would follow him to the office any chance I had, doing my best to learn as much as I could. From the age of ten until the time I graduated from college, I only wanted to do one thing. I studied finance at Auburn University and even served as president of the business school my senior year. Not only was I was involved on campus, but my summers were spent as a door-to-door salesman. I knew my dad was in the relationship business and that it wasn't easy to convince strangers to hand over their money. I figured I would engage in the most extreme form of sales I could think of to prepare for the rejection that was sure to come. What an experience! My summers were spent in Kalamazoo, Michigan; Farmington, New Mexico; and Eau Claire, Wisconsin. My rookie summer I lived with my student manager along with one other student from Auburn. We stayed with a family in their personal home and spent our days going door to door, selling homework instruction manuals. You know, it was definitely one of the craziest things I had done up to that point in my life, but I was good at it. I finished the first year at the top of our sales organization and decided I would participate again this time as a student manager. Over the course of my sophomore year I learned how to recruit other students to join my team. By the end of my third summer I had built an entire sales organization consisting of fifty students, each with their own sales territories. Did I mention that I was only twenty-two years old? (There's much more on this experience in the later chapters.) This opportunity did wonders for my confidence and I could not wait to graduate and start my career as a financial advisor.

I graduated in the spring and went straight to work for a regional firm, experiencing early success. I was doing great and having so much fun, and things continued this way for the first five years of my career. In late 2007, the investment capital markets took a dramatic turn for the worse and my business suffered tremendously. During this market correction I had a major gut check that caused me to rethink my role as a professional investment advisor. As you can imagine, I had more than a few angry clients who demanded (and rightfully) a legitimate explanation. That was a very tough time, but I managed to conjure up the intestinal fortitude to continue. The next five years were completely different asI experienced significant growing pains. I received an education in the school of hard knocks. I had to rethink the way I viewed the investment markets. It took three or four years, but I found my stride again. By 2012, I was back at it with fierce abandon. It's funny how life works out though. No sooner had I pulled myself out of my professional funk, which had been brought on by the Great Recession of 2008, did I have an opportunity of a lifetime drop in my lap. Before I share this next phase of my career, I want to remind you that I was now ten years in as a professional advisor. I had built and rebuilt a solid book of business that was spinning off recurring revenue. I guess you could say I was comfortable. But if I stayed comfortable, you would not be reading this, as I would never have gained the inspiration and passion I now have to share.

In the fall of 2012, I was given an opportunity to build a salesforce for a company I absolutely adored. The founder of the company was a personal hero of mine, so needless to say, I was ecstatic. This was an investment-related company, so there would be some parallels to my career a financial advisor. It would mean, however, that I would have to walk away from the business I had spent ten years building. This was a decision that I could not have been more excited to make. Sure, I was comfortable. At that point I had been married for five years and had an expanding bottom line. Change was staring me straight in the eye and I had to make a decision. Although I was extremely grateful for the experience and the relationships built as an advisor, I was focused more so on the possibilities of an unproven path. At the time of this writing, I am one year into my new role, and I can honestly say that I love every day for the new adventure it holds. My role had not existed before, and our company has grown organically by choice for the last twenty-five years. We are trying new things, some of which work great, others that fail miserably. The thing I love most about this transition in my mid-thirties is that now I know how to do it and have the incredible advantage of perspective. My plan changed and I went with it. I'm not suggesting you get up from your desk tomorrow, hoping for a new and grand adventure. What I am saying is be open minded to whatever may come your way. So what's the most important thing you can do at this point? *Get started and dismiss the details.*

CHAPTER 5

What are You Waiting For?

Time waits for no one: so what are you waiting for?

—Scottie Somers

You never know how your plan will go until you live it. Have you experienced your first detour? Have the wheels come off yet? Remember, a plan is only as good as the action it calls for; you don't have the luxury of knowing when the surprise will come! To apply what you already know and put it into action is where it becomes challenging. Your plan is not the destination but a means to a temporary end. Even if you discover your passion on the first go-around, you need to get comfortable with starting over—even though starting over stinks. I'm not saying that the pursuit is going to be comfortable, but then again comfort is not the goal. There is no urgency in comfort. Complacency is a killer created by fear and insecurity. These are emotions we all experience, but we need not let them paralyze the pursuit. Although you'll never know exactly how your plan will go until you pursue it, you can certainly start over at any point along the way. If you wait until your plan is perfect, you may be comfortable, but you won't be fulfilled. There is a great catastrophe in life that we conveniently label the comfort zone, but it carries the capacity to cripple you. We excuse our inactivity with socially acceptable tags like "creatures of habit" or "routine rangers," living with the attitudes of "if it ain't broke don't fix it." Our comfort zones are fabricated, though; there is no truth involved. We construct them with our illusions of control. In order to overcome this mind-set, we must anticipate change and aim for more than comfort. The more appropriate attitude should be this: "If it ain't broke, it will be!"

Life is a roller coaster and we are not at the controls. Anxiety, frustration, and disappointment appear when we try to control outcomes rather than activities. We do not have the luxury of defining outcomes, but we do decide what we do each and every day. Let's revisit my sickness as a young teenager for an illustration on how devastating control can be. By the time I turned sixteen, I had been sick for three years straight. I was weak, malnourished, and extremely self-conscious. So I did what any normal teenage dude would do. I hit the weights, and I hit them hard! Pumping iron became my new release, and it was just refreshing enough to redirect my thoughts away from the constant pain.

Unfortunately, lifting weights was not enough to satisfy my newfound interest. Soon I was thinking about lifting everything I could. I had become a muscle-head and was convinced that nothing was too heavy for me to lift. I used to play mind games with myself, rationalizing that I was weak if I couldn't lift anything and everything in my sight. I would mow the lawn each week with a backpack full of books. I remember holding a wooden napkin holder shaped in the form of bull over my head as my family ate dinner together. I would sneak into the bathroom in the middle of the night with my hand weights so I could lift in quiet solitude. This particular ritual didn't last long, as my mother caught me one night. She explained that she'd heard a loud, disturbing noise coming from my bathroom, which had led her to investigate. I was horrified when she opened the bathroom door at 3:00 in the morning, but what could I do?

In my mind I was no longer the scrawny and weak little kid with a terminal illness. I jumped to the complete opposite side of the spectrum. If there was a way to portray a tough and macho image to anyone with a pulse, I was all about it. What in the world was I thinking? I surely didn't know; I just figured these were things that all tough guys did, and I wanted so desperately to be one. I was developing an obsession. I'd approach my parents and lift them off the ground. I would walk by my bed and lift the legs off the floor. I was crazy, but I couldn't stop. This new obsession of mine had completely shifted my focus away from my disease, which in and of itself was a great thing. The devastating part of this mind shift was the mental imbalance I had developed.

The kids at school started to notice my erratic behavior as well. I couldn't see it, but I was clearly distracting my classmates as I tried to lift my desk every five minutes while class was is session. The beginning of the end came during the week of final exams my freshman year. What I didn't know at the time was that I had been reported to our guidance counselor. I will never forget what I was doing that landed me in a psychiatric clinic. I'd decided that since my behavior had become so disruptive in the classroom, I would remove one of the desks from my history class and take it to the bathroom. Imagine! I was actually curling that very desk in the boys' bathroom while I was supposed to be taking a final exam!

I was caught in the act of my most ridiculously obsessive behavior and there was nothing I could do or say to defend my actions. There wasn't one thing normal going on in that bathroom that day, and the sentence laid upon me was very well deserved. When my mother arrived at school, she was escorted to the guidance counselor's office where I sat waiting. I had no real desire to defend my actions, so I just stayed quiet and and listened. The guidance counselor explained what had happened, and my poor mother just lost it. Her emotion triggered even more emotion from me. The only way I was going to finish my freshman year was if I agreed to be checked into Norton Children's Hospital's psychiatric ward. The counselor described my erratic behavior to my weeping mother. He concluded that my actions were not normal and said I would benefit from intensive therapy. Well, as you can probably imagine, I was dead set against this idea. I hated the counselor for even suggesting something so preposterous. My mother had no choice but to agree. After all, I did have to pass the ninth grade.

The course of action that followed was anything but graceful. I had been sentenced, and there was no way around this trip to the funny farm. Despite this realization, I did what any irrational, rebellious teenager would do. I fought tooth and nail. I kicked and screamed the entire way there. My dad had to physically place me in the car and restrain me on the way to the hospital. I cried the entire drive over and was bound and determined to attach myself to the seat of the car so as not to be admitted to this nuthouse. Again my dad had to physically remove me from the car. I have no idea how he managed to get me up the elevator and into the custody of the medical staff of Norton's Children's Hospital and then all the way up to the fifth floor. As soon as we walked through the door, we were greeted by a nurse who would take me to my room. I took one look at her, and in a fit of rage I lifted her as high as I could in the air. She was a bit surprised by my move, but my parents were horrified. That single act of defiance solidified my presence in the psychiatric clinic.

There was no question that I'd developed a serious behavioral disorder, and it was up to the Norton medical staff to work it out of me. I was taken to my room, and as I looked back, my parents were walking the other way and out the door. At that very moment I felt more abandoned and betrayed than ever before. The nurse was as kind as she could manage to be, despite my attitude toward her. My new room was about as lonely and stale as I could imagine. There was a bed, a sink, and a bathroom. This was no four-star hotel by any stretch. The nurse left the room, and I seized the opportunity to lift my bed just to see how heavy it was. Much to my delight, it was not heavy at all, so I continued lifting it up and down. It took about thirty seconds for the nurse to come right back into the room; she just looked at me and shook her head.

I was officially checked in to the hospital on a Sunday afternoon around three o'clock. My shoelaces were taken away along with anything in my suitcase that was even remotely sharp. I was in a certified crazy hospital, and these measures were all part of the check-in process. I had no interest in dinner that night and certainly not in meeting any of the other patients. I went to bed feeling more dejected than I could ever imagine. I wanted nothing more to do with my parents. As far as I was concerned, they had dropped me off for good.

Those first few days in the hospital were horrible. I was forced to wake up and interact in group therapy sessions. My world was rocked as I listen to the other kids talk about how they had tried to kill themselves and the pain they had felt for so long. I kept thinking to myself that I had to get out of there—and fast. I was surrounded by a bunch of suicidal lunatics, and I began to fear for my safety. I resisted every part of the therapy, convinced that I was just fine. Halfway through the first week my mother came to visit, and as soon as I saw her, I ran and fell in her arms with a face full of tears. I begged her to take me home, but it was no use. Her short visit did more harm than good, as it caused even more bitterness to arise in my heart. I was in a world of pain and hurt, and my attitude was horrendous. I don't know what it was exactly that caused my mind to open, but all of a sudden I began to embrace my place in that hospital. Obviously there was something wrong with me, or else I wouldn't be there. I was the only one who thought my presence in that hospital was a bad idea. I also figured that if I had any hope of ever leaving that place, I had better start to cooperate. I began to open up to some of the other kids in the program. It's funny how things started to get better as my attitude improved.

I woke up Thursday morning with a renewed sense of humility. I was scared, but I was ready to start the healing process. I couldn't believe how well my disease had been acting, as I had relatively no digestive problems during my time in the hospital. The first group therapy session that morning was my opportunity to speak about my obsessive compulsive disorder. I tried my best to articulate to the group why it was that I felt the need to lift everything in sight, and suddenly I felt accepted for the first time since my obsessive behavior had begun. It was as if those other kids in my group knew exactly why I was engaged in this behavior. The more I spoke, the better I felt. Soon I wanted to hear about everyone in that place. A stone had been lifted from my heart, and I was fully engaged in the treatment that had been so strongly recommended. Maybe it was the comparison that made me feel much more normal. Listening to other kids describe how they had tried to kill themselves was terrifying, but I had compassion for them. The more I listened, the less I thought about my own disorder. I can now see the healing power of group therapy is in surrendering completely. The less I focused on myself, the better I felt. Surrounding myself with people who were struggling with the same things was completely and totally refreshing. Those next three days flew by, and I actually began to enjoy myself. The interaction with my doctors was also taking a turn for the better. More and more I opened up and answered questions, allowing them to make more informed decisions related to my treatment.

The official diagnosis that I received at the end of my stay at Norton's Children's Hospital was obsessive compulsive disorder. I had no problem with the obsessive part, but compulsive disorder? I guess I could see how feeling the need to lift everything in sight was a problem, but disorder seemed like such a harsh word. I learned that my disorder (OCD) was one characterized by unwanted and repeated thoughts. I hated the little voice in my head that told me I was weak if I didn't try to pick up the refrigerator. I learned that the compulsive part of my disease was the action of lifting whatever was in my sight. I would do the actual lifting in order to get rid of that voice telling me I was weak. The remainder of my time in the hospital was spent listening to my doctor explain how my compulsions would provide only temporary relief from my obsessions. My problem was not necessarily rooted in lifting random objects but in the obsessive thoughts that were constantly running through my mind. I was taught to realize these obsessive thoughts were the result of a rebellion against my sickness. I so desperately hated being sick all the time that I taught my mind how to redirect focus. All of this was the result of my need to control my life.

Expecting change will force us out of our comfort zones, and anticipating change will cause us to pursue purpose and detest mediocrity. There is no question that your plan will fail. The only question is *when*. The only thing that remains constant in this world is the fact that things change. This includes your interests and, in some cases, your talents. We've already established the need for flexible planning in this marathon of life we all live. The ability to pivot when life throws you a curve will allow you to remain firmly on the path to purpose. When you face obstacles, you will decipher opportunities. When you encounter trials, you will create triumphs. Now it is time to give chase and pursue your plan with fierce abandon. Life is hard, but you know that already, so let's get on with the pursuit, shall we?

We talked about tactics for finding peace in the midst of chaos in the previous chapter. Your ability to find comfort in otherwise uncomfortable situations will ensure that your flexible mentality will strengthen. So how do you run a race without a predefined start and finish? Currently, the earth contains six billion people. You are only a small part of creation, but this does not diminish your need to run the race. Life happens in the pursuit of purpose. Your race is unlike any other, which makes your destination unique. The destination is your purpose and the path is what you make of your pursuit. So how do you know what you're supposed to do with your life? I can tell you from personal experience that if you're still guessing, it's not too late to start over.

Your pursuit will be unique, so resist the urge to compare. We are all at different points at any given time along the way, comparison will only bring discouragement and discontent. The important thing is that you are accountable. Maybe you assemble for yourself a personal board of directors. You give a few select individuals access to your plan and grant permission to scrutinize your actions (or lack thereof). I've found that when I share my plan with anyone who is further down the path, it makes me that much more determined to follow it. And speaking of taking action, it's important to remember than *now* is all you have. This moment will soon be gone—will you take advantage of it? Time is the most precious commodity, and we all have the same amount. Do not put off for tomorrow what can be done today. Last year I heard a particular sermon that hit me like a ton of bricks. The message, which covered something called *someday syndrome*, was all about the power of *now* and the pitfalls of procrastination. I remember the message as if it were yesterday, and it led me to a belief that inactivity is arrogance disguised as apprehension. There is no such thing as later. Next week doesn't exist, and for that matter, tomorrow may never arrive. As long as you believe in *later*, you will continue to live with the someday syndrome. For trivial matters of life this might not be such a big deal. But why would you practice what you do not intend to pursue? Now is your next single step. You cannot procrastinate in the present. It is all you have. Resist the urge to get bogged down in details. Pick one thing and get to it. Next, forget the rest! That's right. Keep your focus narrow and do what you can now. This is not the moment to contemplate your plan. You do not need the distraction of comparison in the present. Now is for action and not for analysis. Take care of the moment, and the matter will take care of you. And remember, you do not have to go at it alone. Chances are you know someone who has walked a similar path and is waiting to impart that experience. Do you have the audacity to ask?

The pursuit most certainly has the capacity to wear you down. Failure and frustration on a regular basis can lead to physical and mental exhaustion. It is important to remember that your pursuit is not necessarily a solo journey. Think about where you are with your plan. Can you think of anyone in your circle who may have walked a similar path? What if you were to contact that person and ask for help? Would that be such a bad thing? Life is hard enough, particularly if you are trying to reinvent the wheel. Chances are your plan is an innovative derivative of an existing idea. If you could save time and energy while you honor the accomplishments of a predecessor by asking for guidance, why wouldn't you? There is no question that you alone must learn from your mistakes, but you can also learn from the mistakes of others—that is, if you have the courage to ask for help. Help is essential to both your creativity and longevity in life. Help removes the pressure from your efforts alone and leads to collaboration through community. There comes a point in every man's life where his desires change from making to mentoring. Would you rob an old man of his joy by refusing his input when indeed it could be just what you are missing? I love the famous quote of legendary football coach Vince Lombardi, "Fatigue makes cowards of us all." So what's your view of help?

We have thoroughly discussed potential and the plan. Potential is where you determine your efforts should be spent. The plan is the journey to move you from where you are now to where you desire to be. The pursuit is the action behind the plan. You now know your talents and interests and have an idea on what to do with them. Fantastic! You're on a roll, but you cannot stop now. Without movement, your plan is nothing more than a theory. It might work, but then again it might not. You will not know until you go! Another way of looking at pursuit is practice. Are you actively engaged in practice? Think about your daily life and record your activities. Could any of these be classified as practice? Perhaps you have a workout plan that calls for a certain amount of time on certain days. You have the potential to lose weight, build muscle, or complete a marathon. Your plan is designed to help you accomplish the task you have chosen. Your pursuit is the daily practice of working out. Your pursuit must be consistent. This much you know. There is a reason that health clubs across the country experience a surge in new activity during the month of January. New Year's resolutions are a product of intentions, but they do not last. The typical New Year's resolutions are based upon performance or appearance and not purpose. These goals only address the outer layers of personal development. In others words, the why just isn't big enough. I'm sure you've heard the expression, "If your why doesn't make you cry, then it's not big enough." If you are not personally convicted, you will walk away at the first sign of struggle. You will not sustain the setback to see if a setup even existed. The main reason to establish a why is to hold yourself accountable to your pursuit.

The outcome of pursuit is based on the price you are willing to pay. The cost is unbearable for most and is precisely why the majority of the population will settle for ordinary. Life is simply too short to settle. In the words of Jim Rohn, "Suffer the pain of discipline or suffer the pain of regret." I love how Rohn uses the word discipline in this profound statement. After all, we are currently addressing the third step in a disciplined process designed to uncover purpose. Unfortunately the majority of the world lives in a constant state of regret. Goals are set but never accomplished. Intentions are manufactured but left undone. According to a January 2014 study conducted by the University of Scranton, two of the top ten New Year's resolutions had to do with losing weight and staying healthy. The study also found that 45 percent of Americans regularly make resolutions, and of those 38 percent are related to physical appearance. Sadly, only 46 percent of resolutions are maintained beyond six months.[15]

Resilience is a wonderful byproduct of failure. Resilience is not possible without blood, sweat, and tears. The bigger the cost you are willing to pay as you pursue your plan, the more likely your resilience will be manifest. What's the point of finding your purpose if you cannot appreciate it? Setbacks, obstacles, threats—these are all key ingredients of your pursuit. You will discover the chance to turn these setbacks into setups, obstacles into opportunities, and threats into triumphs—that is, as long as you are prepared to start over as many times as it takes. You see, there is no formula. You won't ever have the luxury of knowing how many pursuits you'll have to make. If that's what you're looking for, I am truly sorry. If that's what you're looking for, I'm not sure how much good the rest of this book will do you. There are certain tactics that can stack the odds in your favor, but there are certainly no guarantees. You're just going to have to ask yourself in this moment, "Am I willing to find my passion no matter the cost?" Remember, I found my passion lying on my deathbed, so if you have a will, I can tell you from my own experience that there is a way.

Let's revisit our discussion on potential from chapter 3. Your interests and talents can have tremendous influence on your pursuit. Think of these areas as your strengths. Let's say that you are a great communicator and that you have a genuine interest in meeting new people. You plan to run for public office in the near future and understand the importance of mounting a grassroots campaign. You will now plot your pursuit based upon your strengths and work your plan accordingly. You understand that your candidacy for public office will depend upon the

---

15 http://www.statisticbrain.com/new-years-resolution-statistics/

full engagement of your potential. Therefore, you plan to meet and remember at least one person per day for the next year. You anticipate days that you will fall short and account for that in your overall plan. If the year calls for 365 new friends (names and all), rather than holding fast to the daily quota, you adjust to a monthly number of thirty. You can now pursue your plan with fierce tenacity! The likelihood that you will follow through is very high because your activity is centered upon your strengths. Your pursuit now becomes a matter of building upon your strengths and outsourcing your weaknesses.

Now, I do not believe that there is such a thing as a well-rounded leader. I know it sounds nice, but it's just not practical. In December 1998, Gallup stirred up a global conversation on the topic of strengths when it unveiled the results of a thirty-year research project. The study concluded that spending time building strengths was far more productive than trying to improve upon weaknesses. One of the most startling conclusions of Gallup's research was that there was no one strength that all good leaders possessed. Moreover, the most effective leaders are not well-rounded at all but instead are aware of their talents and use them to their advantage. Gallup scientists surveyed more than one million work teams, conducted more than twenty thousand in-depth interviews with leaders, and even interviewed more than ten thousand followers around the world to ask exactly why they followed the most important leader in their lives. What they found was that the most effective leaders were always investing in strengths. In the workplace, when an organization's leadership fails to focus on individuals' strengths, the odds of employees being engaged are a dismal one in eleven (9 percent). But when an organization's leadership focuses on the strengths of its employees, the odds soar to almost three in four (73 percent).[16] When leaders focus on and invest in their employees' strengths, the odds of each person being engaged goes up eightfold.

Pretty compelling, huh? Let's face it. There's a reason why you

---

16 http://www.gallup.com/press/113536/press-release-strengths-based-leadership.aspx

label certain character qualities or behaviors as weaknesses! No one is perfect, and there is no such thing as a perfect plan; however, we know that already. Your plan is far more likely to be executed if your pursuit is centered upon your strengths. There is nothing worse than a great idea without implementation. Even bad ideas can lead to brilliance if we are willing to take that test drive. You cannot steer a parked car. It just won't happen. You will not make it to California by driving east, but you can adjust as long as you are willing to start over! Your pursuit is and will always be a series of starts and stops. The quicker you move, the faster you can adjust. The more you adjust, the more resilient you will become. Your purpose up to this point has taken you on a journey that began with surrender, uncovered your potential, pivoted your plan, and plotted the pursuit. Are you having fun yet? Hold on tight because now it's time to hurry up and … wait! Patience is one of the most precious patterns in life. It is a virtue and must be built. Before moving on, it's important that you understand the proper projection of your pursuit. By now you've discovered a kink in your plan. My hope is that you've started again and that you are all the wiser. I cannot promise your detour will lead to a different result, but I can promise that patience will be a part of the picture!

CHAPTER 6

The Worth of the Wait

Patience is passion tamed.

—Lymon Abbott

Time is…Let's see, it could be "money" or "everything" or time could even be "of the essence." If timing is everything, then patience is the only thing. But I hate to wait! I am an action-taker and prefer to see immediate results. The problem with this mentality is that once again it places me at the center, making me completely responsible for the outcome. We have already surmised that more often than not outcomes are uncontrollable. So why would I continue use to place emphasis on matters that are beyond my control? Is there really such a thing as a patient pursuit?

I admit for a second time now that I am living bound by the illusion of control. Impatience is a manifestation of unaccepted helplessness. Even though I've danced with death, I struggle with this to some extent every single day. Deep down I believe that there are few things I have complete control over in life, but I'm certain that my actions do not always reflect that. Patience is a virtue and should be mastered sooner rather than later in life. Patience when practiced professionally is a true work of art!

Patience is extremely difficult in this fast-paced modern world. We are the only country in the world that stands in front of a microwave oven and says, "Hurry up!" Let's consider the source of our impatience, particularly since the state of our society hasn't always been this frantic. No, I remember when I was a young boy and would spend entire days with my retired grandfather during the summer. He worked for fifty years in the auto parts business and retired to a structured life of hobbies, one of which was spending time with me. I would wake up and ride my bike to his house early in the morning, filled with anticipation. We would eat breakfast and then move to his garden, where he taught me how to till dirt, plant, and harvest. He even showed me how to shoot unwelcome varmints. After our time together in the garden we would head in for lunch and then move to the bedroom, where he would turn on the radio and fall fast asleep. Those were the best days of my childhood, and I wouldn't trade them for anything.

At some point along the way things changed. The pace of life picked up, and rest and relaxation lost value. Perhaps it was a product of the Internet and electronic mail. Maybe the shift occurred when cell phones became more prevalent and mobile communication increased in popularity. Or perhaps it occurred when the focal point of entertainment became more self-centered. Whatever happened along the way on the technological frontier certainly began the demise of patience. Technology has given us the idea that instant gratification is possible and that we do not need other people in our daily pursuits.

According to a March 2012 blog post by Eric Dye, there are more than three billion Google searches conducted each day, which answer thirty-four thousand questions per second. However, when questions are not answered quickly, people ask less, and Google found that slowing search results by just four tenths of a second would reduce the number of searches by eight million per day. And it gets even better (or not). One in four people abandon a webpage that takes more than four seconds to load, and 50 percent of mobile users give up if the page doesn't load in ten seconds. From the mobile perspective three out of five people said that they would not return to the site that took more than ten seconds to load. In the United States, 25 percent of mobile users search online with their phones alone. Yes, these people do not have the time to open their laptops or bring out their tablets. Are you kidding me? Amazon. com makes roughly $67 million in sales each day and could potentially lose up to $1.6 billion per year because of a one-second webpage delay! Outside the virtual world but also included in this blog report, Dye found that 72 percent of Americans eat fast food at least once a week. Of that percentage, the majority would not wait in line for more than fifteen minutes! On in five people admitted to being rude to someone that served them "too slowly."[17]

Personal communication skills are suffering while technological proficiencies are growing at warp speeds. Why would a teenager ever need to engage another in an actual face-to-face conversation? Why would a college graduate need to practice interviewing skills? There is no need. After all, isn't there an app for everything these days? I would argue that as long as technology continues to improve, our patience will continue to suffer. In no way am I suggesting that we do away with the Internet or our smart phones, but I do feel the need to raise awareness of the damage that impatience brings.

Waiting is more than a worthwhile effort. When it comes to this essential stop on the path to purpose, there is no hurrying up. Patience often carries a negative connotation because of its perceived passivity. I can understand this viewpoint. At least initially I could. Before my near-death experience, patience was detestable as far as I was concerned. The idea of sitting around and doing nothing just didn't seem productive or practical for that matter. It was not until I survived a near catastrophe that my appreciation for patience began to grow. I am confident that I would have never arrived at the destination of my purpose if I had never learned to wait on it! So before I go on in an effort to settle your skepticism, let me be clear what patience is *not*. Patience is not complacency. Nor is it laziness. Patience is not hoping without activity. Patience is not settling for less than your dead-level best. Get my drift? Patience is not for those who tried once, failed, and then gave up.

Donna Rae Smith believes wholeheartedly in the value of patience.

---

17 http://churchm.ag/instant-results/

In an April 2012 article written for *Smart Business Magazine*, Smith wrote,

> Patience is a lost virtue but it does matter. The benefits we gain from patience are unique; there is no substitute for it. Patience puts us in the right frame of mind to put ourselves in the other person's shoes.[18]

Patience is a hub on your highway to purpose, and there's no way around it.

You do not necessarily learn patience. Patience is developed over time, and grief, disappointment, failure, and rejection are key components. Patience can be an action, but more often it manifests as a reaction. Someone cuts you off in traffic, and then you have a choice. You are sitting at the head of the board room, and the keynote speaker is thirty minutes behind. What do you do? You are positioned at the kitchen table with your ten-year-old son, explaining the multiplication tables for the fifteenth time, and it's just not sinking in. These are hypothetical situation that serve the valuable purpose of practicing patience. So let's consider some practical tips for practicing patience. For starters you could add perspective to daily interactions. If you sense tension in a conversation, you can do your best to see the situation through the eyes of the other person. There is also great power in an open mind and giving others the benefit of the doubt. Listening is another great practice when it comes to exercising your patience. Resist the urge to speak. Rather, ensure that the other person has adequate time to voice concern. Facial expressions can also go a long way. The power of a genuine smile and lighthearted attitude can have an incredible effect on the practice of patience. Last but certainly not least, always be quick to accept responsibility. The next time you face an interaction that tests your patience, evaluate the situation carefully and be fully prepared to

---

18 http://www.smartbusinessblog.biz/leadership/40-the-bright-sider-of-change/621-the-benefits-of-patience

accept fault or blame. As we will see later in the story, patience is an opportunity to evaluate your purpose.

Now that we know the perils of impatience and the promise of patience on a general level, let's move into the application as it pertains to its place on the path to purpose. At this point we are well on our way on that journey to purpose. We have surrendered to the notion that perfection is impossible but also agreed that it does not have to be. Beyond this initial point of surrender, we began our walk first with potential, being the difference in where you are now and where you would like to be. We can then discuss the necessity of a flexible plan in giving yourself the freedom to start over at any point in time and your pursuit, which is the intentional action you take toward making your plan a reality.

The fact that I am now talking about patience may appear to be out of place, but stay with me. A critical component of purpose not previously discussed is character. Have you given much thought to this consideration? A mentor of mine once said that reputation is who you want the world to think you are and character is who you really are. Sobering thought, huh? Character is built in the unknown, when plans don't work out and when failure is more frequent than desired. Patience is the common denominator of such predicaments in life. In this imperfect world life will go wrong. That much is inevitable. It is precisely in these moments when patience will keep you on your path to purpose. I have found that it is much easier to practice patience when I remember that there are very few things in this life I can control. In my moments of vulnerability I have developed a motto that has served me well. "Lose your cool, and you're a fool. Learn to wait, and you'll do great!" I hope you will make it your own.

Another critical component of patience is faith. We will not always be able to see the effects of our actions. We can work efficiently and consistently toward a goal without seeing visible results. I think back to the old movie *Karate Kid* when Mr. Miyagi is teaching Daniel the art of defense in a very nontraditional manner. Daniel shows up day in and day out, hoping to learn karate. Each day Mr. Miyagi has Daniel perform some random act of manual labor. He starts by painting the fence and then moves on to buffing the car. Unbeknownst to Daniel, he is inadvertently learning how to defend himself. The specific arm motions he uses to paint the fence and buff the car are the same actions that are necessary to block oncoming punches. The climax comes one day when Daniel has finally had enough, and he voices his complaints. In that moment Mr. Miyagi throws a punch and Daniel subconsciously blocks it. Mr. Miyagi throws another, and the result is the same. Daniel simply "paints the fence" and "buffs the car." Daniel simply blocks it. Mr. Miyagi throws another to defend himself. If you've seen the movie, you know that Daniel has the chance to fight and utilize all the skills that Mr. Miyagi taught him over an extended period of time. In the end Daniel turns out to be an accomplished martial artist, but it would not have been possible without patience. Purpose is undiscoverable without patience, and your attitude will have much to do with how you personally handle adversity. Accepting adversity as part of the package will ensure that your patience grows stronger, leading you more directly to your purpose in life.

In summary, we know that life is not easy and that adversity is a normal part of life. So much of our ability to overcome everyday setbacks is centered on our mind-set. In her book *Mindset*, Dr. Carol Dwyeck talks about the two types of people in life—those with a closed mind-set and those with a growth mind-set. Closed-minded people are quick to defend themselves, believing that their abilities are fixed and have no potential to develop. These are the people with the greatest tendencies toward impatience and intolerance. On the other hand, those with the growth mind-set see adversity as advantageous, preferring to view setbacks as setups and obstacles as opportunities. Every point of criticism becomes a classic case for growth. These are the people who are unshakable, incapable of being discouraged. As a result, these are the people who have the capacity for the greatest amount of patience. These people are most in touch with their need for improvement and devote themselves to development with the greatest patience possible. Think about it. If you are not currently where you want to be, then what are you going to do about it? Well, a close-minded person would throw up his or her hands and resign, believing that there is nothing that can be done. Growth-minded people live constantly in that gap between where they are and where they want to be. As a result, these people are filled with optimism for finding their ways, which requires patience.

Patience is most certainly not the destination, but it is a necessary stop. I spent the first twenty-six years of my life on the wrong path, half of those years spent riding the sick train. I had no idea what patience meant. I could not be bothered by anything other than feeling well. In hindsight I realize this was a devastatingly selfish period of life that should have killed me. I was a miserable human being who was incapable of thinking about anything other than my pain. I was demanding, rude, and impatient. I realize that my actions wreaked havoc on the ones who loved me most in the world. It took this season to get me to realize that life does not revolve around me. I was an extremely sick little boy, but that certainly did not give me the liberty to act the way I did for so long. My sickness alienated me from my friends and family, and it even led me down the path of obsessive compulsive disorder. I'm not so sure that I would have been mature enough to follow my own advice about patience during that period in my life. I would not wish those years on my worst of enemies, but a valuable lesson was learned indeed. Patience is one of the most difficult virtues in life, particularly for dominant personalities like mine. Nonetheless, it is absolutely essential to navigate life with passion and purpose. I love the ancient proverb that reads, "All good things come to he who waits." I can honestly say that my life today is living proof of the truth found in this passage. There is no reason in the world that I should be alive today. My life ended before my very eyes on a cold Canadian operating table, but God was not finished with me. Since that experience in March 2006, I have learned the value of patience and have experienced a life beyond my wildest dreams. I want this for you as well. You've just got to give it (whatever it may be) time to develop.

CHAPTER 7

It's Gonna Hurt

Do you not see how necessary a world of pains and troubles is to school an intelligence and make it a soul?

—John Keats

There is so much good that results from pain. Pain comes in all different shapes and sizes. As a culture, we have been programmed to avoid pain at all costs. Anything that could possibly lead to discomfort is a bad thing. Not only do I disagree, but my life also disproves this theory completely. I have had the wonderful advantage of living more than half of my life with a physical disease characterized by chronic pain. In the beginning I was bitter and played the victim. I did not understand or appreciate the fact that it was happening to me. I had a stomachache more often than not. I spent upward of eight hours in the bathroom each day. There were periods when my stomach would hurt so badly that I could not stand up, much less eat. I share these details because of my current outlook on pain. (Remember how I started this chapter!) In my short life I have come to the conclusion that pain is a choice and not a feeling. Let me repeat that because I want to make sure it sinks in. *Pain is a choice, not a feeling.* This chapter will speak directly to the benefits of pain and the necessity of overcoming it in order to find your purpose. We live in a cold and harsh world where pain is everywhere. That being the case, I want to encourage you to expect and anticipate so that you are not devastated when it comes. For thirteen years of my life I let pain get the best of me, and it nearly put me in the grave. There is no reason that you should experience the same struggles and this chapter is an effort to protect you against the possibility.

I realize that my personal story is a bit of an extreme case. In no way do I expect you to relate to a near-death experience, but at the same time I do not feel you have to in order to develop the resilience to overcome pain and adversity. Looking back, I now consider myself fortunate to have been diagnosed with a chronic illness at such an early age. I believe this because I have never known how to take anything for granted. My personal struggle with pain for so many years helped me build a profound appreciation for all things in life, including adversity. I learned that pain is a matter of focus. It is inevitable; there is no way around it. What you do with your pain will influence your outlook on life.

My hope is that I will be able to communicate the fact that pain is little more than a blessing in disguise. If there is any way that I could have anticipated the life I am living now in the moments of my greatest sickness, I would have been much more pleasant to be around! The fact is, pain has the potential to hijack our attention. We do not mean for it to be this way, but when pain strikes, our concerns are directed inward. Think about the last time you cared for a sick friend or family member. Was that a pleasant experience for you? At the same time, do you think your sick loved one enjoyed barking orders and sending you on a wild-goose chase? In my moments of greatest pain I did not intentionally seek to cause my parents distress. It was all I could do to make it through. In the moment, pain steals care and concern for others, but fortunately it will not last—that is, unless you allow it to. The blessing of pain is the gratitude left behind, but it is a matter of choice.

There are two perspectives worth examination when it comes to the effect pain can have on us all. There are those who assume the role of victim and see to it that everyone suffers along with them. Victims complain about their pain but do nothing to correct it. Victims are content to suffer just for the sake of it. Victims talk a big game, but do not have what it takes to overcome. This was me for the first ten years

I suffered with Crohn's disease. I had a tangible out in surgery, but I blatantly refused as it was just too much to bear. It was not until my body literally shut down that I experienced the most incredible blessing of my entire life! I draw this comparison because in my heart of hearts I do not want you to have to experience a similar emergency. On the other side of the picture there are those who experience pain and overcome it while they achieve victory. The victor is the person who becomes stronger, more determined, and more resilient as a result of pain. Victors by no means enjoy pain; they simply use it to their own advantage. Once I was finally able to regain my faculties after six weeks in the ICU, I slowly but surely began my comeback, which was marked by pain and setbacks. This was a different sort of pain than what I had experienced in my sickness, but it was still pain nonetheless. The difference was that I had decided to redirect my focus toward the perceived benefits of pain. It all started with a walk around the hospital floor, pushing my IV pole with me. I will never forget that first stroll, and it became the foundation for what I now call a semiprofessional triathlon career! Hey, if I can do it, anyone can.

As we continue down the path to purpose, I would like to suggest that pain is a sign that you are moving in the right direction. If you are still with me, I believe that you are intent on finding your purpose (at least for this season in life!) You are not content to simply be. You believe that you were created for more than what you are currently living. We have discussed the importance of surrender, potential, planning, the pursuit, and patience. Now we have transitioned into a result of these aforementioned steps. This is a practical book, a literal how-to based upon my experiences throughout my first twenty-six years. I suspect that you agree with my premise on pain thus far, but allow me to further explain my conviction on the power of pain in life. It is impossible to experience growth without pain. Growth comes in the face of discomfort. Growth treats setbacks as setups and obstacles as opportunities. Sure, pain is a temporary inconvenience, but the key word is *temporary*. Think of life as a mountain range comprised of peaks and valleys. If the valleys represent pain, then we are either in one currently, have just been through one, or are headed into one. Up close these valleys can look terrifying, but with the proper amount of perspective they are much more manageable. I think we know this intuitively, but in the very moment of our pain, we often react rather than think. Pain is not for the faint of heart, but that does not diminish the reality of its existence. Anticipation can go a long way toward the successful navigation of pain. Remember, pain is fine as long as it is not final. It is perfectly fine to stop there, but to stay there is a literal devastation.

So let's talk more about the necessity of successful pain management. We have already agreed that pain is both necessary and temporary. It is a checkpoint designed to propel you toward your desired destination. You and only you can decide what the destination may be, but you are also the one who must recognize when pain necessitates change. You will never do anything different in life until the pain of same becomes greater than the pain of change. Since we are talking about the benefits of change, I want to focus on potential as previously defined in chapter 3. You are on a journey. You most certainly are not where you began, but you are also not where you want to be. This gap represents the change you desire to make, and you are most definitely experiencing some form of pain. It could be the result of a lack of willpower, inconvenience, or even impartiality. Losing motivation to follow through on the commitment you made could also be a form of pain. These are all temporary and will only affect your progress if you allow them to. These are obstacles and need to be proactively managed, so let's talk strategy, shall we? Let's bring back our New Year's resolutions as examples. We all know that the large majority of resolutions never last beyond the month of January. This is precisely why the pain of change is so strong. It never ceases to amaze how crowded the parking lots are at the gyms throughout January. Inside new faces are frantically working to will new habits into place. The thing about behavior change is that beliefs drive activities.

The way to change any behavior is not simply to start something new but to change what you believe about your new activity. Exercising is a great thing. There is no disputing this fact. In order to successfully maintain a new exercise routine beyond a New Year's resolution, you must anticipate the pain that will surely come along. Some examples include but are not limited to physical pain in muscle soreness, lack of motivation because of incremental progress, inclement weather conditions particularly in the winter months, and other people not in line with your priorities. Perhaps you could write these along with any other interruptions down for the purpose of anticipation. Go ahead and plan your reaction before these things even occur. Having a plan ahead of time will give you more strength to successfully navigate these pain points. Give yourself a little room to slack but then quickly return to your discipline and watch as your resolutions become habits and your habits eventually become a new way of life. It is in this moment that your pain of same became greater than your pain of change. Success breeds confidence, which in turn creates momentum. Celebrate the small victories along the way and watch with wonder as you transform your body into a newer, fitter version of yourself! Oh, but do not stop there. You are starting to figure out how to navigate through your pain, so keep going.

You have a choice when it comes to pain, and it is not whether or not to experience it. You can allow pain to work you, or you can work your pain. We are born with an instinct to avoid pain. This is a natural defense mechanism that we learn early in life. I remember putting my hand on the motor of a running lawnmower. I can say that I have never done anything remotely close to that since that time. I learned a painful lesson one day as a five-year-old boy, but that pain was absolutely necessary. I experienced pain but then successfully navigated around it. In this particular example I was able to make pain work for me. It would be an entirely different illustration if one day I decided to burn my hand on a lawnmower motor and then continue to do the same day after day. I start with this example because it is very clear in making a point. Of course, I do not want to suffer second-degree burns to my hand on a regular basis. The choice beyond that first experience was obvious. If I did not wish to experience the same physical pain over and over, I should not put my hand on the motor of a running lawnmower. It seems as if physical encounters with pain are much easier to avoid the second time around as we usually learn our lesson the first time. I often wonder why we cannot see the painful reality that accompanies a life of mediocrity. By mediocrity I mean anything short of full engagement in your vocation, with family, and at play. I wouldn't think twice about keeping my hand off a hot lawnmower motor simply because my first experience was met with pain. I am pretty sure that if you had a similar experience, you would feel the same way. If you have a thing for physical pain, that's your prerogative, but please allow me to make application to other areas in life.

We were created for a purpose, and my purpose with this book is to help you find yours. If all you are doing is surviving and doing what is necessary each day to get by, then you are most definitely riding the pain train. To steal from my previous illustration, you are burning your hand day in and day out by repeating an action that you know will result in pain. Why do you continue to do it? You continue on your painful path of life because it is predictable. At this point in your life, your pain of change is greater than your pain of same. You are terrified of what might be, so you continue on the path of predictability. You have settled and become content with mediocrity because it is familiar. You have willingly confined yourself within the corners of your comfort zone, thereby limiting your potential. At some point along the course of life, you resigned to your dream. It is precisely this underwhelming climax that provided me the inspiration to write this book. It is this mind-set that represents a catastrophic flaw in mankind and will most certainly lead to obscurity. It's as if we grow numb to the pain of everyday life and accept it as routine. Forgive me, but I'm not okay with that. As a matter of fact, that is nothing more than "stinkin' thinkin'" that will keep you exactly where you are for as long as you live. It also represents the victim mentality, and you becoming a slave to your pain. By continuing to live in your painful present, you are giving up hope for what could be.

Am I striking a sensitive chord just yet? Are you a tad bit upset at this point in the book? In case you haven't picked up on my premise thus far, I am not interested in your comfort. I believe that if you have read this far, you are at least open to the potential benefits that finding your purpose might bring. We have addressed five stops on the purpose path, including surrender, potential, pursuit, plan, and patience, each requiring a mastery of its predecessor. Up to this point each stop has required self-examination and introspection. Now that we are on the topic of pain, the tone has taken a bit of a shift. Pain is a part of everyday life, but it can represent a catalyst for explosive character development and personal growth. Pain has the potential to do great things in your life, but you have to be willing to take corrective measures. You cannot continue to tolerate pain by settling for a life devoid of meaning. You must be honest with your feelings and your current outlook on your life. One very simple way to identify this is by asking yourself, "Am I excited about going to sleep tonight so that I can wake up fresh to a brand-new day?" If your answer is anything other than an enthusiastic yes, your current level of pain might be greater than you are even aware. I would encourage you to stop reading. Yes, put the book down and go outside. Think about what you have learned this far about the path to your purpose. Think about the practical advice and the specific direction given thus far. Do you have it in you to engage this path and start to make it a reality in your life? If you cannot bring yourself to start (and notice how I said *start*, for your focus should be in the now), then I would ask you to reflect on your life up to this point. As you continue to walk, ask yourself what the world would gain if you were living a life of purpose.

You only have one life to live, and it won't be perfect. Pain is a sign of imperfection but stopping there is a surefire way to guarantee that you will never find your purpose. Pain is a blessing in disguise, but it requires recognition followed by corrective action. In order to make your pain work for you, you must decide that your current situation has to change. There is nothing comfortable or easy about change, and we are born with a natural resistance to anything that remotely resembles the notion. Nevertheless, if we cannot learn—and I do feel this is a skill that can be learned—to adjust in the face of pain, then we will be overcome again and again, making excuses for the rest of our lives.

Different does not have to be devastating, but for some reason it often is. Our routines rob us of opportunity, and most of the time we don't even know it. The first step toward differentiation is incredibly simple but extremely difficult at the same time. Living by the "If it ain't broke, then don't fix it" mentality will ensure that we never move away from the familiar. Familiar is fine if all you want out of life is comfort. Differentiation will challenge you. It can be mastered, but it requires a daring discipline. Anxiety and uncertainty are sure to follow, but eventually your new outlook will become what was formerly known as routine. By now we are well into the details of this discipline, but for the purpose of inclusion into this specific segment on pain, let's refer to it as "your route to stand out!" When it comes to standing out, pain can be a great indicator that you are doing something right.

Standing out is hard. Standing out is scary. Standing out will require an unwavering commitment once the decision has been made. It will not be fun, and it won't be easy; however, if you keep going no matter how hard things get, you will find your way out to the other side of authentic purpose. Or you can continue to ignore the pain of a life that is less than your absolute best. Pain can do you so much good if only you move in the direction it points. There is no doubt it will rouse you to stir. The only question is this: Do you have what it takes deep down in the bottom of your soul to move? It took more than thirteen years and a trip to the emergency room that saved my life to open my eyes to the life-changing benefits of pain. What started as purely a physical transformation has evolved into an entirely different mind-set. You see, whenever I'm uneasy or feel a bit out of place, I am assured that I am exactly where I need to be. I have learned that true character growth can only occur outside the friendly confines of the comfort zone. I have also learned that the comfort zone is a temporary illusion of satisfaction and fulfillment. Most importantly, my dance with death has taught me that I do not always know what is best for me. The longer I live with a closed mind, the more likely I will be to snatch defeat (which represents impartiality) out of the jaws of victory (which is purpose).

Now that you are aware of the reality of pain on your way to purpose, you have a choice to make as to what you will do with it. Your pain will result in either paralysis or perseverance. I do not intend to sound insensitive, and the last thing I want to do is offend. You might be experiencing an extremely challenging season of life and have more pain than you know what to do with. I have been there and want to be as sympathetic as I can be. The words you are reading are coming from experience and the collection of advice sought from others who also have gone through epic seasons of pain. What I hope is to provide encouragement and the know-how on navigating through this season of pain you are currently experiencing. Perseverance is a choice, but it might not feel like the most desirable one in the moment. I would not be alive today and writing this book if I had not found the strength (and not all of it was my own) to embrace the pain of my physical transformation and allow it guide me to a remodeled mind-set. As I said before, if I can do it, anyone can, and the remainder of this book will show you how.

CHAPTER 8

A Relentless Requirement

"The brick walls are there for a reason. The brick walls are not there to keep us out. The brick walls are there to give us a chance to show how badly we want something. Because the bricks walls are there to stop the people who don't want it badly enough. They're there to stop the other people."

—Randy Pausch, The Last Lecture

How badly do you want it? Your purpose is out there somewhere, but are you willing to find it? Remember, pain is your compass. Moreover, have you decided on the front end to remain resilient no matter the cost? Desire is not something that can be taught. Perseverance is the gateway to passion. Once you have found your passion, you will find you are living in the center of your purpose. There's more on passion in the chapters to come, but I need to dangle the carrot now to paint the picture for what lies on the other side of perseverance. For the time being, we must roll up our sleeves and reinforce our commitment to pushing through the pain. Pain represents the great divide and will be the differentiator of whether or not you decide to continue your path to purpose. Every moment of pain represents an opportunity for perseverance that can result from an interaction or self-imposition.

Think about your day and retrace your steps, beginning with the time your feet hit the floor until the moment you closed your eyes. Awareness must precede assessment, which will ultimately lead to corrective action. I'd recommend keeping an activity journal either electronically or by notepad. Record your thoughts as you experience the day. What conversations did you have, and what words expressed caused you pain? In the context of conversation pain can come in many shapes and sizes, including but not limited to frustration, disgust, embarrassment, and annoyance. Whenever you encounter these types of emotions, write them down. Be sure to include the environment and the details of your surroundings. Record your overall mind-set leading into the conversation. It is imperative that you are fully aware of the conditions that cause you to experience pain so that you know when perseverance might be required. A reaction as a result of a painful experience most often leads to more of the same. You do not have the luxury of choosing the actions and/or words of the other person, but with practice, you most certainly can control your response. Wouldn't it be great to enter any conversation with the confidence of complete and total self-control!

It is also important to give consideration to the impact your own thinking has on your overall sense of well-being. You may find the trajectory of your sub-conscience is causing you to experience pain. The mind is an incredibly powerful machine, but you do have the ability to harness it. Think about the specific environments that arouse negative thoughts. How might you be able to reshape your outlook toward these specific conditions? The very practice of overhauling your natural tendency is a classic case of perseverance. Before long you will begin seeking out potentially painful situations solely for the purpose of practicing perseverance. According to the beliefs of the US Navy SEALs, you will always default to your current level of training. If you want it bad enough, you will execute the small things that lead to the large payoff. By learning to identify your consistent pain triggers, you can begin to build your relentless resilience, which will reinforce perseverance. Practicing on the smaller things of everyday life, such as human interaction and negative thinking, will lead to increased confidence as the stakes get higher. The closer you get to your purpose, the more crucial perseverance becomes.

Let's continue on the topic of our thinking. Pain plus transformational thinking equal perseverance. I worked as a door-to-door salesman during the summers of my college career for the Southwestern Company in Nashville, Tennessee. The mission of the company is to "build character in your minds." One of the many tactics utilized in accomplishing this mission was the relocation program. The company guidelines were as follows: Those students living in the South region of the United States would relocate to the North to work for the summer, and those students living on the West Coast would relocate to the East Coast and vice versa. Considering I had attended college in the state of Alabama, I spent my summers in and around the Great Lakes. The sum total of training for this extreme sales adventure exists in a one-week conference known as sales school! As you can probably imagine, motivation is of the upmost concern and priority. I can honestly say that as a young adult I was exposed to the most talented and dynamic leaders in the entire sales profession. It is on this specific matter that I continue with my illustration.

Mort Utley has to be one of the most renowned figures in the sales industry. He single-handedly redefined the insurance sales cycle. Mort recognized that insurance was not exactly a glamorous concept. After he successfully developed a relationship-based approach to selling insurance, he created an incredibly powerful and influential speaking platform. I first heard Mort's keynote speech at sales school in Nashville in June 2000. "Remember the pony" was all about the power of positive thinking, which we now know serves as the foundation for perseverance. Mort used the illustration of a pony to represent an insurance sale. He began his speech by talking about two little boys who were locked in a room with a pile of manure for a period of five minutes. One at a time the boys were asked to enter this room. Watching from the observation chamber, the testing agents immediately took note of the first boy as he stood as far from the manure as the small room would allow, clinching his nose firmly with thumb and forefinger. The boy was paralyzed, making not even the slightest movement. It was clear the boy was distraught as the five-minute time limit expired. Mort used the most brilliance of facial expression and gesturing to further accentuate the negative thoughts of the first-test subject.

Then, in a shift of excitement, Mort began to describe the contrasting experience of the second boy. His enthusiasm was nothing short of amazing, and you could hear the excitement in his voice as he told the story. The boy entered the room in the exact same manner as the first boy. The testing agents were dumbfounded as they watched the boy dive into the large pile of manure. The boy continued to dig and flail his arms through the pile until the five minutes had elapsed and the test was over. The agents were scratching their heads in disbelief as they tried to make sense of the differing reactions. It was plain to see what the first little boy was thinking, as his body language said it all. But the second little boy was a mystery that could not be solved without direct feedback. Mort was grinning from ear to ear, barely able to contain himself as he delivered the comments of the second little boy. As a matter of fact, the words that left Mort's mouth next would become the cornerstone on which this speech would be forever remembered. After the little boy had gotten cleaned up, he returned to the observation chamber with the following comment: "With all that poop piled up in one place, there has to be a pony somewhere!" I, along with the other five hundred college students in attendance for the speech, erupted with applause.

"Remember the pony" was a message that shaped my outlook on life forever. It was a picture of perseverance that I committed to memory at an early age. The very next day we left for the sales field with energy and aspirations of grandeur. I am happy to say that after eight weeks of selling homework study guides door to door in Kalamazoo, Michigan, I both encountered and conquered pile after pile of manure. There was the first weekend in a strange area where I asked more than fifty families if I could live with them for the summer. I never will forget the first time I knocked a bit too early and was met with a frown and a shotgun. Oh, and there was the time the police officer escorted me out of a particular neighborhood I was working in because of resident complaints. You'd better believe there was character being built in my young mind! After the second week I called home and wanted with all my heart to quit. I hated the response on the other end of the phone at the time, but to this day I am forever grateful for the ground that my parents stood. There was no way I was quitting, but that was an early sign of the pain that I referenced earlier in the chapter. Every hint of pain is an opportunity for perseverance. It all depends on our perception. When I was finally able to shrug these incidents off and learn to not take them personally, I arrived at a much better place. Those first two weeks in the sales field were absolutely brutal, but I finally learned how to overcome. From that point on each negative reaction served to make my determination stronger. Whenever I would encounter a hostile resident, I would simply tell myself that the person just received some terrible news and thank goodness I was there to shoulder the brunt of the angry response. Because I was there to receive the heat, it prevented the spouse or child of that particular person from suffering the rage at some point in the future. With this new attitude I was unstoppable! I finished my first summer in Michigan and had such a great experience that I elected to return for the following two summers as well. Mort Utley had a tremendous influence on my life; he taught me the invaluable lesson of perseverance.

Another brilliant display of perseverance, one that brings tears to my eyes every time I think of it, is the life of worldwide evangelist Nick Vujicic. Nick was born in 1982 in Melbourne, Australia, without arms or legs. His early days were difficult, as expected. Throughout his childhood Nick not only dealt with the typical challenges of school and adolescence but also struggled with depression and loneliness. Nick constantly wondered why he was different from all the other kids. He questioned the purpose of life. He wondered if he even had a purpose. According to Nick, the victory over his struggles as well as his strength and passion for life today is credited to his faith in God. His family, friends, and the many people he has encountered along the journey have inspired him to carry on as well. Since his first speaking engagement at age nineteen, Nick has traveled around the world, sharing his story with millions, sometimes in stadiums filled to capacity, speaking to a range of diverse groups that include students, teachers, young people, business professionals, and church congregations of all sizes. Today this dynamic young evangelist has accomplished more than most people achieve in their lifetimes. He's an author, musician, and actor, and his hobbies include fishing, painting, and swimming.[19] In 2007, Nick made the long journey from Australia to Southern California, where he is the president of the international nonprofit ministry Life without Limbs, which was established in 2005. Amazingly Nick was married in 2012, and his wife gave birth to a baby boy in April 2013. Nick learned how to make pain work for him, and in so doing, he has positively influenced millions of people all over the world.

Where are your piles of manure in life? How do you deal with pain, frustration, and disappointment? I think it is very clear how the majority of the country's population today chooses to deal with adversity. We have a choice when it comes to pain, and we just discussed the picture of perseverance. This picture, however, is not so pretty, and the result is paralysis or a failure to deal. According to the Anxiety and Depression Association of America (ADAA), anxiety disorders are the most common mental illness in the United States, affecting forty million adults age eighteen and older (18 percent of the US population). Anxiety disorders cost the United States more than $42 billion a year, almost one-third of the country's $148 billion total mental health bill, according to "the Economic Burden of Anxiety Disorders," a study commissioned by ADAA (published in *The Journal of Clinical Psychiatry* in July 1999). More than $22.84 billion of those costs are associated with the repeated use of healthcare services. People with anxiety disorders seek relief for symptoms that mimic physical illnesses. Major depressive disorder is the leading cause of disability in the United States for ages fifteen to forty-four, and affects approximately 14.8 million American adults, or about 6.7 percent of the US population age eighteen and older, in a given year.[20]

Paralysis occurs in the form of mental illness. I am not proud of

---

19 http://www.lifewithoutlimbs.org/about-nick/bio/
20 http://www.adaa.org/about-adaa/press-room/facts-statistics

the fact that I was diagnosed with obsessive compulsive disorder as a teenager, but it does not diminish the fact that it happened. I played the victim by allowing my Crohn's disease to overtake me. I had no interest in surgery that would have corrected the underlying problem of daily stomach pain. I chose to redirect my focus on an illusion that I had created to mask the pain. I convinced myself that I was a bodybuilder and that lifting weights was my life. I refused to live in reality in favor of a world that I had created. It was at that time that I was first introduced to the tragedy of addiction. I had taken a good thing and made it a god thing. Not only did my physical symptoms elevate, but I also managed to create for myself a mental disorder that led to hospitalization and medication. I pretended that my pain wasn't real and developed habits that wreaked havoc on my family and those who loved me the most. It was bad enough that my stomach was always hurting and that I could not seem to stay out of the bathroom, but now I had created a mental war that made me even more sick.

The reason that I am able to speak so adamantly about both sides of pain management is that I played both victim and victor. The premise of this chapter is firmly placed on perseverance, but in order for you to appreciate the sincerity of the message, it is appropriate that you know I can relate to the forty million adults who are suffering from mental disorders. I was checked into a psychiatric hospital and required to live alongside suicidal patients. The experience scared me beyond imagination. I never dreamed that my addiction of lifting would land me in a treatment facility. I was treated in the exact same manner as the rest of the patients. My shoelaces were taken from me and all sharp objects were removed from my room. I am not proud of this particular part of my past, but I feel it is important that you know. If I cannot connect with you on a personal level so that you feel my words are genuine, then how can I ask you to consider following the steps to your purpose that serve as the content of this story?

All I had to do was face my pain and take responsibility for the healing that would be follow. If I could have listened to the doctors and had the surgery when it was first advised, I could have persevered much sooner and began my recovery on a voluntary basis. At that point even though I was suffering miserably, my pain of change represented by the surgery was still greater than my pain of same. I said it before, but it merits being repeated. If I had known that my physical life could be so amazing at the time when the surgery was first mentioned, I wouldn't have resisted for thirteen years. I would have gladly walked into that operating room. You know what they say about hindsight though, and life doesn't work through the rearview mirror. I elected to learn the hard way, but the most important thing is that I did eventually learn. So how can you possibly benefit from my near-death experience? I simply ask that you read these words and give careful consideration to the trajectory of your life in relation to the pain you are currently struggling with. Maybe you will read something that resonates and decide to take corrective action. After all, time is your most precious commodity, and today is the first day of the rest of your life.

Without perseverance there is really no place else to turn. Avoidance is a tactic that only lasts for so long. Think about a small argument you have had in the past. A small disagreement can escalate to a heated altercation. You may have been the aggressor, but if you were the suppressor and chose not to retaliate in favor of running away, chances are there was collateral damage. At the same time, if the pain could have been addressed in the precise moment when it occurred, it would not have been so damaging. On the same topic, medication is not a long-term solution. There is nothing reasonable about that $42 billion per year industry. Depression and anxiety disorders are real; I don't dispute that whatsoever. I simply suggest that confronting pain and taking responsibility for the residual affects might provide a more long-lasting benefit.

Pain is an incredibly powerful phenomenon. We discussed the modern-day miracle of a man born without arms or legs who lives an extraordinary life to this day. Unfortunately Nick Vujicic is the exception. This is a big, dark, cruel world, and we will never be able to escape the reality of pain. My hope is that you will begin to view pain in a different light. Rather than asking, "Why me?" might you consider asking, "Why *not* me?" Furthermore, when you shed the victim mentality and adopt responsibility in whatever form it may come, you open yourself up to perseverance. When it comes to dealing with pain in my life, my outlook now is this: "If not me, then who? If not now, then when? If not pleasant today, then passion tomorrow. If I have no pain, I have no gain."

I believe with all my heart that if we can learn to anticipate pain, we can learn to appreciate it as an opportunity for perseverance. We have considered both sides of the pain train—the victor and the victim. You do not have the luxury of choosing whether or not to experience pain in life. That comes as a product of the world we live in. You do, however, decide what you will do with your pain. I tried both methods. When my Crohn's disease got so bad that the pain was beyond tolerable, I convinced myself that it wasn't real, and in so doing, I developed an anxiety disorder that required psychiatric treatment. I do not recommend that path. Finally, against my will but necessary to save my life, the surgery I avoided for thirteen years was finally performed. After a brutal recovery I discovered my passion and am now living my athletic dream. There's more to come on my passion in the next chapter, but let me assure you that the later action is much more desirable. I would confidently recommend that path! Perseverance is more than worth the pain, and I can promise that you will love what awaits you on the other side. I know it hurts, but pain is temporary. Pain is weakness leaving your body, and passion is forever. Now it's time to have fun. Passion is your playground!

CHAPTER 9

Passion Pays

Nothing great in the world has ever been accomplished without passion.

—Georg Wilhelm Friedrich Hegel

Congratulations! You have officially arrived! You have most definitely fought tooth and nail, shed blood, sweat, tears, and probably lost hold of your sanity on more than one occasion. But if you are still reading, there is one thing I know for certain. You decided before you ever began this process that the payoff was more than worth the struggle. I say again that you have found your passion. Passion is something we were all born with but so few of us actually live. It is much easier to see in the younger version of ourselves. Passion takes risks without worry of consequence. Passion speaks of possibility rather than reality. Whereas the preceding steps on this path to purpose might not have been so straightforward, this is a step we can all relate to without any instruction. The problem is that we have allowed the world to throttle that which makes us feel most alive. Rather than pursuing passion with fierce abandon, we opt for the socially acceptable versions of ourselves. This is no way to live, but sadly most of us fall into it.

Need more convincing? Just consider the divergence between work and play. Does there really need to be a difference? Why does work have to be a grind, a necessary evil? Why can't passion be found in the workplace? If we weren't so concerned about perfection and living the lie so that the world might perceive us as having everything together, we might just be able to treat work and play as one in the same. Why are we obsessed with the practical? Sadly we value conformity over creativity. You are the only person on the face of the earth who can do what only you can do. Yet we insist on finding the path of least resistance, the one that allows us to blend in rather than be ourselves.

According to an article in the October 2013 issue of *Forbes Magazine*, there are twice as many "actively disengaged workers as those who are fully engaged. The path of least resistance (the one that allows us to blend in rather than be ourselves) is becoming more and more popular. The latest version, which was released this week, gathered information from 230,000 full-time and part-time workers in 142 countries. Overall, Gallup found that only 13 percent of workers feel engaged by their jobs. That means they feel a sense of passion for their work and a deep connection to their employers, and they spend their days driving innovation and moving their companies forward. The vast majority, some 63 percent, are "not engaged," meaning they are unhappy but not drastically so. In short, they're checked out. They sleepwalk through their days, putting little energy into their work. A full 24 percent are what Gallup calls "actively disengaged," meaning they pretty much hate their jobs. They act out and undermine what their coworkers accomplish. Add the last two categories together, and you get 87 percent of workers worldwide who, as Gallup puts it, "are emotionally disconnected from their workplaces and less likely to be productive." In other words, work is more often a source of frustration than one of fulfillment for nearly 90 percent of the world's workers.

In the report, Gallup breaks the numbers down geographically. The findings are striking if not surprising. I won't run through all 142 countries, but here is a sampling. The highest levels of disengagement, what I'll call people who hate their jobs, are in the Middle East and North Africa. Given the civil war in Syria, it seems predictable that 45 percent of people would be desperately unhappy at work. But in Algeria (53 percent) and Tunisia (54 percent), workers are even unhappier. As far as happy workers in those countries, Syria had zero. Algeria had an impressive 12 percent, and Tunisia just 5 percent. Qatar made the best showing with 28 percent happy, 62 percent mildly unhappy, and 10 percent hating their jobs. I would have thought that Israel would have more happy workers, but only 6 percent are engaged. Moreover, 73 percent are checked out, and 22 percent hate their work.

The lowest proportion of happy workers is in East Asia, where overall just 6 percent of workers are engaged. That number holds for China, where only 6 percent of employees are happy in their jobs. Some 68 percent are checked out, and 26 percent are very unhappy. I find the numbers for Japan surprising. I would have thought there were more happy workers there too, but only 7 percent, which is just one percentage point better than China, are happy in their work. Sixty-nine percent are not engaged, and 24 percent hate their jobs. In Latin America, the biggest economy (Brazil) has the happiest workers. An impressive 27 percent are engaged. Still 62 percent are disengaged, and 12 percent really don't like their work. Brazil's numbers are better than any country in Western Europe. For instance, in France, only 9 percent really like their jobs. Some 65 percent of people are checked out, and 26 percent are very unhappy. Germany is a bit better with 15 percent happy, 61 percent not engaged, and 24 percent actively disengaged. It turns out the United States has some of the best numbers in the world with 30 percent happy in their work, 52 percent feeling blah, and 18 percent who hate their jobs. Those numbers are not what we would want, but they are better than most places. Where do the happiest workers live? They live in Panama, where 37 percent love their jobs, 51 percent are not engaged, and 12 percent are very unhappy.[21]

Why is it so hard to live your passion in the place where you need it most, namely the workplace? The matter is simple yet devastating. As a society, we are not passion-oriented. Passion is not practical so we have to prepare ourselves to pursue it no matter how silly it appears to the

---

21 http://www.forbes.com/sites/susanadams/2013/10/10/
unhappy-employees-outnumber-happy-ones-by-two-to-one-worldwide/

world around us. We may look silly along the way, but once we arrive, we can be sure to stay.

Up to this point I have provided instruction with regard to successfully navigating each step. Intuitively you were already aware of the importance of surrendering to the concept of perfection, identifying your potential as to where you want to be, preparing a plan to get there, organizing a pursuit simply by starting, developing patience, anticipating and accepting pain, and deciding ahead of time that you were going to persevere no matter how much it hurt. Passion is the natural result of a relentless dedication to finding the thing that only you can do. The purpose process thus far has involved a deep dive in self-reflection. You have experienced ups, downs, and all-arounds. The path to purpose is not one that ends in perfection, and that notion alone could be hard to swallow.

So now let me ask an extremely sobering question of you. What have you determined your passion to be? You and only you can decide, and if you don't, the world will do it for you, thus confining you to mediocrity. Let that sit for a moment as you contemplate the areas of life that give you the most satisfaction and a sense of accomplishment. One thing is for certain. You care enough about something to put up with pain. Pain is too … well, painful to endure without a commitment to something greater. Passion is what makes the pain worthwhile and keeps you in the game. Without it you will always quit at the first sign of struggle. Both our minds and bodies are resilient, but we must tell them to be so. Pain is the body's natural defense mechanism, and it alerts us to potential danger. Stress acts in the same way but has more of a detrimental effect on the mind. Passion directs both pain and stress but only if we choose so. Passion connects us to our purpose, and that is precisely where we desire to live. Desire is not enough though. It takes deliberate and intentional effort. This effort will come only as a result of conviction and unrelenting focus.

Passion is the intersection between your calling and enthusiasm. You care enough about something to have come to the point where you can rest in your imperfection. As you struggle through the messy middle, which lies between your potential and purpose, you will experience imperfection at its finest. But that is one major reason you care. You are not concerned with achieving perfection. Rather, you know that this area of your life does not have to be perfect, yet your desire is not deterred. I trust that you are on to what I am trying to conjure up in your brain by now. The problem with perfect is that is often paralyzes potential.

I hope by now that you have found this book useful in guiding you to your passion no matter how long it takes. It is perfectly okay to not be okay. It is just not okay to stay that way. There is nothing wrong with starting over. Why do we feel that vulnerability is unthinkable? Speaking from personal experience, I have found that my greatest strengths have come as a result of finding peace with and not being afraid to showcase my weaknesses. There is strength is weakness, even as counterintuitive as that may sound. Knowing the areas of your life that need improvement is tremendously beneficial because it identifies a starting point. The point at which you identify your potential is the point that allows you to begin the process. As we learned with step two, pursuit is doing the first thing to move toward your potential—not five things, not all things. The first thing is the most powerful. You would never know that a gap exists if you were not aware of the weakness in your life. Starting over is essential, and you might have to do it consistently for an extended period of time. The worst thing you can do is pretend that your weakness is not there. Rather than addressing the areas that need improvement, ignoring them will only ensure that you continue to blend in. Ignoring your weaknesses will further diminish any hope of discovering your passion because it will lead to impartiality where you become numb to your instincts and true feelings.

Passion is not easy to find, but it is possible. You are going to live your life anyway. Why not find enthusiasm, excitement, and energy? Why not jump out of bed every morning, anticipating the adventure of the day ahead? Living a life in any other way is a disappointing waste of time. None of us have the luxury of spending time tolerating our activity. Merely surviving just doesn't cut it. We were created to thrive.

If you aren't living every single moment as if it were your last, you have fallen short of your passion. This is the exhilaration that living with passion can bring. Fully alive is to be fully engaged. I have experienced this phenomenon, and it has been truly amazing. I am living in the center of my passion and could not imagine living in any other way.t

More details on my personal story will come, but for now let me ask you again if you are passionate about your life. What do you think about most? Where do you spend the majority of your time? To steal from the subject of the last chapter, what did you persevere through because you loved it so much? Now where would you spend your time if you had the choice? What might I observe if you were acting out of love and interest rather than duty and obligation? Love and interest are passion ingredients where duty and obligation speak of practicality. Why should you wait until Friday night to come alive? Why can't you have the weekend mentality through the week? All you have is your time and this moment. Are you passionate, or are you practical?

Let me set the record straight before I proceed. In no way am I suggesting drastic measures. Please do not walk into work tomorrow morning and announce to your boss that you are through! That would be the wrong type of passion, the kind that results from emotion. Here's another point of caution as you contemplate your passion: Feelings are not always reliable. Your feelings are often triggered by events outside your control. It's perfectly fine to express discontent over your current situation, but you should do so in confidence and in a way that leads to corrective measures. For example, let's say you're an accountant working like a madman through tax season. It is the first of April, and the deadline is only a few weeks away. Late on Friday afternoon your boss presents you with a complex case that requires your immediate attention. Your first thought, "I really need a break if I'm going to make it through this last week of tax season. You even went so far as to plan a special evening with your wife at your favorite local establishment. Unfortunately, you now "get to" work late which will continue into Saturday. What a joy, right? Okay, first take inventory of your emotions and try to control them. Next, consider your options while you continue to control your emotions. There is no question you are angry and frustrated. Your elaborate plan is blowing up in your face and you have a decision to make. It is in this moment that self-control can save your job and salvage grace that will be needed when you deliver the news to your wife.

It will do you no good to react in an emotional tirade because of an isolated incident that might not ever happen again. You can express your anger and frustration, but you should do so in a constructive manner and in the company of your wife, not your boss! After you bring your pity party to a close, start to plant seeds elsewhere within the world of accounting. Again, it will do you no good to complain if you do not intend to rectify the situation. Discontentment should lead to dutiful diligence, not to depression.

Okay, now that the disclaimer is out of the way, let's get on with the journey. We've considered perseverance and pain. We have discussed the importance of developing a plan and pursuing it sooner rather than later. We have also looked at the tremendous value of surrendering to the notion of perfection while redirecting focus to potential that ultimately leads to purpose. With each chapter we have analyzed the role of the stops along the way. The intent has been to build momentum and create clarity so that you (after careful introspection) have a course of action that will lead you to your unique purpose in this life. We are now unpacking passion because ultimately when you find it—and I believe that we all have a responsibility to do so—you will have found your purpose. The thing to remember at this point is that passion is not necessarily a singular focus. In fact, you probably have more than one, and they might not even be related. That's no problem. By no means are you limited. The only limitations you might face are the ones you place upon yourself with a narrow focus. I am passionate about triathlon and serving kindergarten school kids at church. I have friends who are passionate about singing country music and gourmet cooking. It really is a matter of your own creative genius with movement toward the development of these interests.

Once you have discovered the path, you can very easily find your way back. Think about the first time you ventured outside your own familiar geographic territory. Perhaps it was your first road trip or crosstown adventure. Before you started, the destination was unknown; however, once you took action, momentum took over, and you eventually found your way. The same can be said for passion. In this case passion is the destination, and the first time you search it out, you would be best served by following the recommended path. You start with surrender and then hang a right at potential. Potential leads you through a roundabout to a plan, and from there you take the fork left toward pursuit. From there you head due west toward patience, which points you toward the exit ramp known as pain. The only way to make it through the town of pain is by taking the one-way street called perseverance. If up to this point in your journey the navigation is successful, you will arrive in the thriving metropolis of passion. The first trip is always the hardest, but thank goodness for experience. The first trip will be long and tedious and may not begin until you are past your prime. Ultimately the path to purpose will become familiar, which is why you must find detours along the way. Your ability to reinvent the path will ensure that your passion is renewed as often as you need it to be.

Passion gives no regard to the concept of *prime*. Passion occurs only when you decide to take action. Passion results if and when you initiate. Perhaps you were born with a certain talent but without an interest. Maybe your early interests were in athletics, but you lacked the necessary skills to excel. In the early stages of interest your desire will overshadow your ability. Eventually your talent will catch up but only if you give it the necessary time to develop. This is when repetition becomes so valuable. Doing anything over and over without immediate gratification is challenging; however, repetition leads to confidence, and confidence paves the way for mastery. Remember, there is nothing wrong with starting over except for the fact that we do not do it enough! Maybe you stood for hours in the driveway, shooting free throws, or perhaps you sat at the piano for what seemed like an eternity, practicing. I'm not about to tell you that practice makes perfect; that would contradict the very premise of this book. What I am saying is that in the absence of talent, time and commitment must carry the load. You will get there, but it may take much longer than you would like. Anyone can start, but without focus and determination fueled by passion, the end result will never be fully realized. You may think you are passionate about many things, but the only way to know for sure is to put it to the test. Do you really have what it takes to follow the path thus far? In simpler terms, do you know what it is that you enjoy, and can you articulate it in a way that causes others excitement?

If not, you might as well start thinking, but that's not the only thing you should do. Thinking is fine, but acting is essential. Thought without action will take you nowhere. The last thing this world needs is another brilliant thinker! You can think passionate thoughts, but if you stop there, you will only experience frustration. You have to put your passion to the test by trying new things. Maybe you love the Cooking Channel and one day decide to step into the kitchen to create your own masterpiece. Perhaps you feel strongly about the mission of Big Brothers/Big Sisters and make a commitment to serve in a formal capacity for a defined period of time. These are the types of actions that will either lead you to or away from a perceived passion. Thinking you might enjoy something is much different than moving into that something and experiencing it firsthand. Only you can determine your passions. If your passions exist only within your mind, you might as well dream for the rest of your life. I hope you wake up soon, as I know the world will be a better place with you living in the center of your passion.

One last characteristic of passion is that it might not always play fair. Often your passion speaks out of place. Sometimes your passion breaks the rules. Sometimes your passion will get you into trouble, and sometimes your passion must ask for forgiveness rather than permission. As we mentioned earlier, passion is most definitely not practical. I would be remiss if I did not take this moment to share my favorite quote of President Teddy Roosevelt, which is taken from an excerpt of his speech "Citizenship in a Republic" he gave in Paris, France, on April 23, 1910.

It is not the critic who counts; not the man who points out how the strong man stumbles, or where the doer of deeds could have done them better. The credit belongs to the man who is actually in the arena, whose face is marred by dust and sweat and blood; who strives valiantly; who errs, who comes short again and again, because there is no effort without error and shortcoming; but who does actually strive to do the deeds; who knows great enthusiasms, the great devotions; who spends himself in a worthy cause; who at the best knows in the end the triumph of high achievement, and who at the worst, if he fails, at least fails while daring greatly, so that his place shall never be with those cold and timid souls who neither know victory nor defeat.[22]

Practical action is compliant. Passionate action is courageous. Practical plays nicely with others and fits neatly within predetermined boundaries. Passionate action might not always please the world and cares little for coloring within the lines. Practical thinking is easy because everyone else does the same. Passionate thoughts lead to exceptional accomplishments for everyone else to admire. So the question you really must ask yourself is this: "Am I an action-taker or an admirer?" Admirers are essential so that passionate action-takers can be exceptional and create that which can be admired. As long as you are acting within the parameters of legality and not causing physical harm to others or yourself, by all means throw caution to the wind and create your own passionate rules!

Personally I think the content of this chapter is most memorable. If there's one thing that everyone who meets me for the first time can say, it's that I am passionate. My life at this point is a second chance. I have seen what it's like to die. I have danced with death and lived, and so this day (and the ones to follow if they come) is the greatest blessing I could have ever hoped for. You see, I now live with the "If not now,

---

22 http://www.theodore-roosevelt.com/trsorbonnespeech.html

then when" mentality. If I want to make something happen, I have to get started today. This sense of urgency has served to fuel my passion for life. Everything in life is an adventure for me. Every person I meet is a new story to be captivated by. Every trip I take is an opportunity to experience something different. People are absolutely fascinating, and every conversation I have is a chance to bring out passion in an unexpected way. I believe with all my heart that relationships are the only things that last forever in this life. My passion, when it comes right down to it, is people. I have been incredibly fortunate with the platform of triathlon to meet and befriend some amazing people. I love to compete just as much as any professional athlete, but ultimately the sport is a means to an end. I hope one day that you and I have a chance to meet and that you experience my passion personally. I also believe that passion is contagious, and if you are living anything less, I want a chance to rub off on you! My passion has led me to my calling, my purpose. This book is all about you finding *your* purpose, and I sincerely hope that you can relate thus far. After you read this chapter, you should be fully aware of the things you are most passionate about in life. That was my intent. With that in mind, I would now like to welcome you to your final destination. *Welcome to your purpose; I hope you enjoy your stay!*

CHAPTER 10

Your Purpose is Not For You

The purpose of life is a life of purpose for the benefit of those around you.

—Unknown

Perfection is impossible, but purpose is imperative. Now that you have found your purpose in life, it's time to give it away! Guess what? This is not a self-help book. As a matter of fact, I do not believe there is such a thing as self-help. The purpose process as described in this book has been all about you, but the destination has nothing to do with you. The problem with perfection is that it leads to self-centeredness. When we finally discover that it is indeed unattainable, we default to self-pity and typically allow it to last a lifetime. No wonder the world has lost heart. We are all walking around with a "woe is me because perfect cannot be" attitude. As long as we continue to carry this mind-set, there is little hope that we will ever find the starting point that will eventually lead to purpose. Purpose is not about you but rather what you can do for those around you. A life of purpose is one that will lead to complete and total satisfaction according to the well-being of other people. I heard it said once that success is the result of adding value to yourself while significance comes when you add value to others. So do you desire to be successful or significant, and how do you use your passions to serve the best interests of those around you? Let's consider a couple significant lives that have positively shaped the world we live in today.

First and foremost, the greatest leader this world has ever seen came to earth as a servant. The Son of God, Jesus Christ, came not to be served but to serve and ultimately committed the greatest act of service anyone will ever experience. Jesus spent the first thirty years of his life as a productive member of society, working as a carpenter. The last three years of His life were spent in ministry, visibly serving everyone He came into contact with. Not that any other human being could even come close in comparison or worthy of being mentioned alongside, but for the purpose of this illustration I will continue.

In 2006, TOMS founder Blake Mycoskie befriended children in a village in Argentina and saw that they didn't have adequate shoes to protect their feet. Wanting to help, he created TOMS Shoes, a company that would match every pair of shoes purchased with a pair of new shoes for a child in need. In 2011, the one-for-one model was expanded and TOMS Eyewear was launched. With every pair purchased, TOMS helps restore sight to a person in need. One for One TOMS has given more than ten million pairs of new shoes to children in need.[23]

Then there is the most famous skateboarder who ever lived, Tony Hawk. After he received thousands of e-mails from parents and children across America who did not have a safe, legal place to skate, and in some cases were arrested for skating on public property, Tony Hawk decided to establish a foundation whose mission would be to serve this population. He wanted to help them develop quality places to practice the sport that gave them much-needed exercise and a sense of self-esteem. So in 2002, he established the Tony Hawk Foundation, financed the organization with a personal gift, and assembled a board of directors who represented a diverse range of backgrounds and expertise.

Since its inception, the Tony Hawk Foundation has sought to foster lasting improvements in society with an emphasis on supporting and empowering youth. Since 2002, the Tony Hawk Foundation has been

---

23 http://www.toms.com/one-for-one-en

fulfilling its mission to help young people by issuing grants to low-income communities building quality public skate parks and providing guidance to city officials, parents, and children through the process. To date, the foundation has awarded more than $5.1 million to 544 public projects for skate parks in fifty states and $100,000 to support the Skateistan (www.skateistan.com) program in Afghanistan, Cambodia, and South Africa.[24]

Finally there is Truett Cathy, founder of Chick-fil-A. The Chick-fil-A Corporate Purpose is "to glorify God by being a faithful steward of all that is entrusted to us and to have a positive influence on all who come into contact with Chick-fil-A." For the past sixty-six years, the fast-food restaurant chain has built a foundational commitment to service—service to customers, service to franchised restaurant operators and their team members, and service to communities. Cathy believed this begins in the restaurant, one customer at a time. The officers of this company firmly believe in treating every person who comes through the doors with honor, dignity, and respect. They teach it to everyone who comes to work at Chick-fil-A, and it's something that they take with them throughout their careers. Cathy believed that service goes beyond the restaurant doors. Currently Chick-fil-A serves its communities through volunteerism and giving. They also make a commitment to take care of the people who take care of their communities. Cathy felt that philanthropic giving reinforces that commitment to service by helping children and families in need. Ultimately this is what makes Chick-fil-A unlike any other organization.[25]

I know this sounds counterintuitive and certainly clashes with everything society promotes of self-interest, but I say again that your purpose is not for you. Blake McCosky, Tony Hawk, and Truett Cathy were very aware of this truth. As a matter of fact, Truett Cathy was famously quoted as saying, "Nearly every moment of every day we have the opportunity to give something to someone else—our time,

---

24 http://tonyhawkfoundation.org/about/
25 http://www.chick-fil-a.com/Company/Responsibility-Giving-Tradition

our love, our resources. I have always found more joy in giving when I did not expect anything in return." Purpose is not necessarily about power, about fame and prosperity, or about being known. Your purpose will allow you to speak and act with conviction, but the benefits of the discovery will be guided toward others. Service is the greatest purpose that anyone can fulfill, but it's a matter of perception that will make the difference.

How you see your purpose will influence the specific activities you pursue. You may have a passion for performance, but that could easily manifest itself in athletics or community theater or even in a sales capacity. How you serve is not necessarily the critical matter. Rather, it is that you serve. There are more than six billion people in the world today, but there is only one of you. Have you considered how your purpose might uniquely make an impact on the lives of others? How might your passions lead you to the end of yourself and forever open your mind to the abundance of service opportunities that exist in the world today? You can find them in your workplace, at church, in your community, or in places that you might not expect. Again you start with your passion and determine what it is that you feel the world is lacking. From there you employ your passion and take action to engage. What breaks your heart? Is it homelessness, child abuse, human trafficking, or adult illiteracy? Are there organizations in your area that exist to serve these populations? If not, can you bring yourself to start one? This is exactly what Blake McCosky and Tony Hawk did, and the world has been forever blessed. It's not rocket science, but it does take movement and dedication to playing a small part in giving back. In so doing, you will find your purpose in service and bring your passions to a whole new level.

As long as you are paralyzed in your imperfection, you will never be able to see the needs of other people. Self-centeredness is a disease that will forever leave you unsatisfied. You will never be enough, do enough, or see enough, so you will live a life of disappointment. The longer you allow this to continue, the more your natural desires will diminish. Ultimately you will be completely numb and oblivious to the world around you. No wonder we have lost heart. We have become so disenfranchised with our pathetic lives because they cannot be perfect that we have let go of hope. No longer are our daily pursuits meaningful in a way that gives us meaning. So we continue to search for something that will never be found. We lead solo efforts that were never intended to be so and build walls to protect ourselves from threats and to keep our weaknesses concealed. We are unwilling to express our own vulnerability for fear of ridicule or a lack of acceptance. We become obsessed with what the world thinks of us and do our best to showcase a life that is not real. This sets the stage for discouragement, grief, doubt, and skepticism. This is the reason that forty million American adults spend billions of dollars each year on anxiety-related medication. Anxiety is a result of living a life without purpose. If you think about it, there is a tremendous amount of energy required in self-centeredness. Just imagine how productive and influential we could be if we could bring ourselves to redirect.

Can you imagine the trajectory of society today if we shifted our primary focus away from first place and pointed it toward second place? We promote first place to the detriment of our own well-being. We say and hear, "If you're not first, you're last," and, "There is no such thing as second place." Competition is a wonderful thing, as it encourages excellence, but it can also be catastrophic. Competition is rampant in our world today, having gone far beyond the arena of athletics in which it was born. We see it the workplace. We see it in the school yard and even in parenting. Our primary focus is how we can outdo the next guy (or gal). We prepare ourselves to perform and to defend against all potential forms of opposition. This has the capacity to bring out the worst in all of us. Weekly I read where companies pursue hostile takeovers and thousands of employees lose their jobs. Parents far too often engage in shouting matches with referees as they watch their children's little league games from the sidelines. Professional athletes are utilizing sports-enhancing drugs to make themselves stronger and faster all in an effort to capture an edge. This is utter madness, yet sadly it is reality.

So I ask again, "What would our world look like if we promoted second place?" Think about how the world would be different if as much time and energy went into assistance as opposed to performance. What if the ultimate prize every four years was the Olympic silver medal? Not to take away from hard work and determination to claim the top spot, but what if? Let's use a sports analogy to further develop this idea. What if Scotty Pippen was as highly regarded as Michael Jordan? Jordan could very well go down in history as the best basketball player to have ever lived, but he could not have won even a single championship ring without Pippen. Jack Nicklaus won eighteen major championships in a span of twenty-five years. But does the name Angelo Argea sound familiar? Argea served as Nicklaus's caddy for forty-four of seventy total PGA tour wins. When Argea was asked, "Exactly what do you do for Jack?" he replied humbly," He asked me to do two things. When he's not playing well, one, remind him that he's the best golfer out there. And two, that there's plenty of holes left. And finally we recognize Dallas Cowboys running back Emmitt Smith as the NFL's all-time leading rusher, but far less attention is paid to Daryl "Moose" Johnston. Johnston and Smith played together for ten seasons when Smith carried the ball 2,539 times and amassed 11,090 yards. During his Hall of Fame induction speech in 2006, Smith credited his accomplishment to his faithful fullback, "Moose" Johnston. Scotty Pippen, Angelo Argeo, and Daryl Johnston each took their servant's role seriously, and in so doing, they paved the way for records to be broken.

At the heart of second place is service. Having peace in knowing that you prepared and performed with maximum effort and still came up short is service. When you approach the winner and extend your hand in a congratulatory manner, you are serving. A feeling of satisfaction and pride that your opponent accomplished victory is filled with purpose. Competition is a good thing, and I love it just as much as the next person; however, where competition falls short, collaboration picks up. Just think of how much more we could accomplish if we learned to collaborate where we used to compete. In an article titled "Collaboration is the New Competition," Ben Hecht writes, "Leaders and organizations are acknowledging that even their best individual efforts can't stack up against today's complex and interconnected problems. They are putting aside self-interests and collaborating to build a new civic infrastructure to advance their shared objectives. It's called collective impact and it's a growing trend across the country."[26] Asking for help is a skill that we tend to overlook or view as subordinate. With the amount of information that floods the world today, it is impossible to master everything. When we can learn to focus on our passions, which will lead us to our core competencies and thus ultimate purpose, and then outsource the rest, we will be able to lead more fulfilled lives. And the best part is that everyone else will!

Purpose begins when we learn to look beyond our own lives and individual needs. It took me twenty-six years to find my purpose. As you now know, it took a bout with obsessive compulsive disorder as well as a near-death experience to open my eyes. I was so sick from the pain associated with my Crohn's disease that I allowed it to create sickness in other areas of my life. Eventually my pain got the best of me. I caused my family and friends enough heartache to last a lifetime simply because I was so self-absorbed. Pain is selfish, and I was held captive for the better part of thirteen years. The only concern I had was making it to the moment when my stomachache would disappear. If I could live a day where I did not spend six hours in the bathroom, I was happy. With this mind-set and inward focus I had nothing left to give to my parents and little sister and college roommates. I was miserable, and I unintentionally made all those around me miserable as well. Maybe your pain at the moment is physical like mine, but it doesn't have to be. You may not call it pain or even discontent for that matter. But if there is anything in your life that captures a disproportionate amount of focus that does not lead to significance (see previous definition at the beginning of the chapter), you need to regroup and see if you cannot bring yourself to surrender, thus launching your own path to purpose.

At the age of twenty-six, months after winning the battle for my

---

26 http://blogs.hbr.org/2013/01/collaboration-is-the-new-compe/

life inside a Canadian ICU, I discovered my purpose. I determined that my passion was people, and building relationships gave me more joy than anything else. As I regained my physical strength and found my athletic passion in the sport of triathlon, new doors began to open and different types of people were introduced into my life. There is a certain amount of responsibility that comes when you survive a near-death experience. The same nurses that helped me through the healing process were now calling for me to share my story with other patients facing similar challenges. Although I despised the early journey of recovery as a hospital patient, the destination was more than worth the trouble. Ultimately my athletic pursuits brought me to the level of national sponsorship in triathlon, and I gained the media accolades that went with it. This allowed me to interact with other patients in a way that provided hope, inspiration, and motivation. When I visit hospitals and perceive the fear and discouragement that is quite obvious on the part of these patients, I am careful to first connect with empathy and compassion. I relate by showing them my own physical scar from the surgery. I share my resistance and bad attitude and ultimately the epic failure that nearly took my life. From there I simply share what has resulted on the other side of surgery. I tell my comeback story and eagerly anticipate the feedback that is always overwhelmingly hopeful. You see, my platform as a sponsored triathlete became my calling card and led me to my purpose—encouragement! There is no doubt in my mind about what I am now supposed to do with the rest of my life here on earth.

In review of each stop along the path, I have found encouragement to be my purpose. People are my passion. Perseverance was the decision I made in 2006 to overcome my setback of surgery. Pain was the theme of my life for thirteen years as I was patient to endure. My potential, pursuit, and plan did not come until after my life was spared, but I am now fully alive in my athletic pursuits of triathlon as well as motivational speaking and writing. Surrender is and will remain my toughest challenge, but I do it. Even though I fully grasp the fact that perfection is impossible, I often wonder if my actions reflect that core belief.

I am a hypocrite. This much I know. At the same time I do not want to waste a second, and I guess that could come off as an attempt on perfection. Now that you know my story as the sick kid who almost died in a Canadian emergency room because I thought I could actually catch perfection, I want to share what has happened since my life was spared and my discovery of the purpose path was made. I previously mentioned that the sport of triathlon is my passion, and I have been fortunate enough to advance to the level of global sponsorship. I am now living my athletic dream, and I often pinch myself to make sure it's all still real. I'll share how all of it happened, going back to my recovery from life-saving surgery in the spring of 2006.

I had not been home from the hospital for more than two days when I began to receive my first round of visitors. I was not at all excited and made no attempt to show otherwise. It had been nearly a full month since I had eaten anything. My entire colon had been removed along with fifteen gallons of intestinal bacteria. I will never forget my surgeon's description of my abdomen when he first cut me open. He described it as a hostile war zone where everything had been blown to shreds. As a result, upon completion of the eight-hour surgery, he had to leave the wound open on the surface to protect against infection from the inside. I also had my ostomy, which was a reminder of the reason I resisted the surgery for so long, and an intestinal drain to prevent bacteria buildup and the site of surgery. I was alive, but barely. I wanted nothing to do with my new life, and my attitude reflected it. To this day, I do not know how my family kept from killing me or themselves. One friend in particular sat down on the bed next to me, and despite my lack of acknowledgment, he began to tell me about a triathlon race he had competed in the day before. I tried with all my might to remain disinterested, but there was something about his inflection that was intoxicating. By the time he had finished his account, I was smiling. I still couldn't move my body, but I could no longer conceal the enthusiasm that resulted from my friend's story. I will never forget that moment to this day. It was the afternoon of June 7, 2006, when I decided to become a triathlete.

All of a sudden my recovery had a purpose. I quit feeling sorry for myself as I shifted my focus from what was to what could be. Now I did have a hole in my midsection. After all, I had been carved up like a Thanksgiving turkey eight weeks before, but that wouldn't stop me from hoping. My physical strength was improving, and I did my best to determine how long I would need to prepare for my first race. I started with walking to the mailbox and then progressed to a walk around the block. Within a month I was able to jog slowly for five minutes at a time. I asked the neighbor if I could borrow his bike and slowly began to build my endurance as well. Within two months of my friend's visit I was running two miles and biking ten. The last piece to master was the swim. I had to be very careful with my swimming. My large wound increased the risk of infection. It had been now been four months since my surgery, and my wound was healing nicely, so I decided to hit the pool. My first trip was humiliating as I nearly sunk to the bottom. This only fueled my determination, and I vowed to get stronger each day. I continued to swim until my endurance was sufficient. I signed up for my first triathlon and was filled with enthusiasm. I had come so far in my training over the last two months, but more importantly, I recognized the victory that came with embracing the challenge my new life brought.

I won the first triathlon I entered and haven't looked back since. During the past nine years I have competed in more than 150 endurance events. I have raced in seven Ironman events on four continents, including an incredible trip to New Zealand. I have competed in the half Ironman World Championships three times in Clearwater, Florida; Las Vegas, Nevada; and Mont Tremblant, Canada. My greatest achievement came at the beginning of my fourth season when I was assigned to the Timex Multisport Team. Since 2010, I have attracted global sponsorships with many different brands, including Timex, Trek, Powerbar, Newton Running, and BlueSeventy. These amazing companies allow me to pursue my passion with the best equipment in the industry. In 2013, I was named to the USAT (USA Triathlon) all-American class and was notified by Ironman that my performance last year put me in the top 1 percent of my age group worldwide. It has been an incredible ride, and I am now deep into my 2014 season. I have already raced six half Ironman events and one full Ironman. I am living my athletic dream, and my passion grows each and every day. Triathlon has given new meaning to my life, and I never would have known if it were left up to me. It has also served as my platform for living my purpose of encouragement. I have been fortunate enough to launch a speaking and writing career based on my personal story. I have spoken all over the country to hundreds of thousands of people and feel fully alive while I'm on stage. I have written guest articles for numerous health-care publications and serve on the speakers bureau for Convatec International, the company that manufacturers my ostomy supplies. When I write and speak, my purpose is encouragement. I know that by sharing my story, I have the opportunity to serve and impact the lives of those struggling with perfection.

Although triathlon has been nothing short of miraculous, the best thing about my recovery was the introduction to my wife. It was October of 2006, and I was training for my first marathon. By that time I had adjusted fairly well to life with an ostomy and had completed three triathlons in the couple months leading up to this event. I joined a local training group that was put together by the national cancer-based Team in Training. We would gather each Saturday morning that fall to run together. It was during one such group training session that I met Marietta Elizabeth Mahaffey. Marietta was the coach of our particular group, and she was responsible for planning the logistics. As you can probably imagine, I will never forget the first time I saw her. She would later tell me she was shocked by my captivation on that particular day. From the moment I laid eyes on her, I knew she would be the one for me. It was an abnormally cold day in October, and she had a stocking cap pulled down over her forehead. The entire group was huddled around her as she announced the running route for the day with turn-by-turn instructions. I tried my best to play it cool, but it was hard to mask my interest. Upon completion of that run and after everyone else had left the premises, I approached Marietta and asked her if we could meet for some training advice. That was my way of asking her on a date, but it worked just the same. That first date led to another, and well, you know how this story goes. We were married in April of 2008, and I am convinced that my improvement in triathlon would not be possible without Marietta's expertise. Not only was she a looker, but she was a health professional as well. Marietta is one of few dietitians who carry the designation of certified sports nutritionist. She has her own practice where she consults with endurance athletes on all aspects of nutrition. She is a household name in our city, and I could not be more proud. I consider my wife to be a gift for discovering my purpose and accepting the fact that perfection is impossible. My life is not perfect by any means, but with a wife who loves me, a sport that motivates me, and a career that encourages me, it is as close to perfect as perfect can be.

If there is one thing a near-death experience taught me it's that *now* is all I have! My life is a prime example of this observation, and my only regret is that it took me so long to discover it. If there is one thing in your life that is keeping you from thriving, let me assure you that it is *you*. We were born to live great lives in a world filled with opportunities, but they will never be perfect. I am convinced that we are capable of so much more than we believe. If you are simply surviving by trading time for some greater good, I would like to challenge you to change your mind. Yes, it will be scary. Yes, you could fail. Yes, you will question your sense of sanity. But even though it sounds crazy, it might just work!

Whatever the case may be, I am certain your purpose is out there. There is no question in my mind that you have passion; in fact, I actually believe you were born with it. The only question is whether or not you have the courage to find it. Can you bring yourself to surrender and move beyond the disappointment associated with imperfection? Do you have the stamina to identify your potential and construct a plan with patience that will deliver you there? Can you recognize that pain is part of the process and decide ahead of time that you will persevere no matter how difficult the circumstances? If you can answer yes to these questions or even take the first step on this path, you will undoubtedly discover your purpose and live the rest of your life fully satisfied and content in significance. The problem with perfection is that it will never be realized, but the same cannot be said for your purpose. No one can find it for you, but we are all counting on you to find it for yourself. The world will be a better place when you begin to live with purpose. With all the gratitude that I can muster from the depths of my heart and soul, I thank you for spending your valuable time reading this story. If there is any doubt that you are living with purpose, will you consider walking the path to purpose?

REFERENCES

1. http://www.psychologytoday.com/blog/the-joint-adventures-well-educated-couples/201209/how-perfectionism-hurts-relationships

2. http://www.healthline.com/health/exercise-addiction#Overview1

3. https://www.nationaleatingdisorders.org/get-facts-eating-disorders

4. http://www.mouseplanet.com/9365/Of_Failure_and_Success_The_Journey_of_Walt_Disney

5. http://online.wsj.com/news/articles/SB10000872396390443855804577601773524745182

6. http://www.authenticdevelopment.com/_blog/Authentic_Development/post/Surrendering_to_Imperfection/

7. http://www.historynet.com/robert-e-lee

8. http://www.jackierobinson.com/about/bio.html

9. http://www.biography.com/people/lance-armstrong-9188901#related-video-gallery

10. http://www.encyclopedia.com/topic/Tiger_Woods.aspx

11. https://www.discprofile.com/what-is-disc/overview/

12. https://www.mbticomplete.com/contents/Faq.aspx#faq23

13. https://www.jocrf.org

14. http://www.jocrf.org/about_aptitudes/who.html

15. http://en.wikipedia.org/wiki/Mike_Tyson_vs._Buster_Douglas

16. http://www.statisticbrain.com/new-years-resolution-statistics/

17. http://www.gallup.com/press/113536/press-release-strengths-based-leadership.aspx

18. http://churchm.ag/instant-results/

19. http://www.smartbusinessblog.biz/leadership/40-the-bright-sider-of-change/621-the-benefits-of-patience

20. http://www.lifewithoutlimbs.org/about-nick/bio/

21. http://www.adaa.org/about-adaa/press-room/facts-statistics

22. http://www.forbes.com/sites/susanadams/2013/10/10/unhappy-employees-outnumber-happy-ones-by-two-to-one-worldwide/

23. http://www.theodore-roosevelt.com/trsorbonnespeech.html

24. http://www.toms.com/one-for-one-en

25. http://tonyhawkfoundation.org/about/

26. http://www.chick-fil-a.com/Company/Responsibility-Giving-Tradition

27. http://blogs.hbr.org/2013/01/collaboration-is-the-new-compe/

Printed in the USA
CPSIA information can be obtained
at www.ICGtesting.com
LVHW091247210724
785408LV00001B/2